# The Buddha, The Vegan, and You

## Part 1: Meat, Myself and Irony
## From Carnism to Compassion

John Bussineau

Calm Water Publishing
West Bloomfield, 2015

**Notice**

All material in this book is provided for your information only and may not be construed as medical advice or instruction. Readers should consult appropriate health professionals on any matter relating to their health and well-being. The information given here is designed to help you make informed decisions about your health. It is not intended as a substitute for any treatment that may have been prescribed by your doctor. If you suspect that you have a medical problem, we urge you to seek competent medical help. Mention of specific companies, organizations, or authorities in this book does not imply endorsement by the author, publisher, nor does mention of specific companies, organizations or authorities imply they endorse this book. The personal medical information I have shared as a result of changing my eating habits are disclosed as an example of what I have experienced.

# Table of Contents

# Introduction

Billie has just called for me. Groggy, I get out of bed and come down stairs, watching and listening. Gabe is having a difficult time breathing yet is still very calm. Cristina is singing Halleluiah to him in an angelic voice. Billie is next to her accompanying. They are letting Gabe know it's OK to go. That we all love him so much but it's OK. *"It's time to go honey, we love you, go to the angels, go run in the fields that you see, we will see you soon, we will never be parted from one another but it's time to leave."* I turn to get some slippers and return. Upon my return he is gone. We say our goodbyes to him. We touch him, stroke his limp body, tell him we love him and hold him one last time.

Gabe, our 120 pound Rottweiler/Dalmatian rescue, died nobly at 12:06 am on Tuesday, October 12, 2010 with his family around him. It was a four-day process starting when he decided to stop eating. We had shared our lives together for ten years and he taught us all lessons on devotion, peace and love. His dignified death process was the last lesson which he bestowed upon us. He was brave and courageous, and while we had a veterinarian on call, he never seemed in pain and just flowed with the dying process. We, his human family, were with him every step of the way and even with his last dying breath he was connected with us and in relationship looking for the presence of his pack. His death galvanized my innate knowledge and confirmed non-speciesist Buddhist teachings that animals are no different than we. As anyone who has ever had love for a companion animal knows they have intelligence, emotion and affection, especially when they greet you upon your arrival home. They are playful and they are sad when scolded. The can be protective, nurturing and are always there to listen, alert, and present. Like us they feel pleasure and pain. Like us, they suffer. And they, like us, do not want to die and will cling to death until the last moment. Gabe did not want to leave us. He didn't want to die and he clung to life for as long as he could and finally let go with assurances from his family around him it was "OK" and "we love you." I learned, viscerally that day, each and every sentient being is the same. Each finds life precious, and each suffers. In this light, our precious Gabe was not different than any chicken, pig, cow, duck or fish. He was no different than any human being. But it wasn't until I stopped eating sentient beings for a few months that I made this pure noncognitive transcendental connection.

Being overweight with high cholesterol, triglycerides, sugar levels and blood pressure I was on the road to heart attack, stroke, and diabetes. I was the "Standard American" eating the standard American diet as well as a long time Tibetan Buddhist student and lay practitioner. I had a veil of delusion covering my core beliefs and actions when it came to the food I was eating. I was on my way to happily killing myself, all the while sitting on my cushion meditating on love, compassion and wisdom. I was killing untold numbers of sentient beings without knowing it and without the knowledge that those sentient beings did not need to die on my behalf. I was unaware that the beings I was causing to be killed, which I ate every day, were also killing me. I was an unknown participant in structural violence against not only animals, but also against the poor, myself and the entire planet.

This book is about how I brought about awareness to these issues, changed my habits, improved my health, and ended my support of structural violence in relation to animal usage (no longer eating them, wearing them, and using products tested upon them, nor going to entertainment using them). This writing is for anyone who would like to explore change for themselves and attempt to have the inner you be more consistent with the outer you. This book is for you if you pray for all sentient beings in the morning and would like to stop eating them for breakfast, lunch and dinner.

This book shows that it is possible with a little effort, to utilize meditation and change a lifetime of bad eating habits. If I can do it anyone can. I have learned through my Buddhist studies that we as humans have the capacity and capability to do anything. If we can become enlightened we can certainly become vegan. This book is about how personal honesty, motivation from my family and the support of my wife helped me to become a better person, healthier and happier, and more the individual I always wanted to become. It's about how I changed after being in a rut for fifty-five years of life and sharing with the reader some insights I have found along the way which perhaps can help you also change, if you choose to do so. It's about my own heath improvement. It's about improving my meditation practice. And it's ostensibly a book about helping all animals, all people and the entire planet. It's about connecting one's inner Buddha nature with one's outer activity thus becoming a more genuine person for all. So if you are interested in improving your health, meditation practice, self-image, and deepening your compassion through exploration of Buddhist thought from a vegan perspective this book is for you.

# 30-days, Seriously?

I came home on the night of April 25<sup>th</sup> 2010 and my wife Billie, who had been talking to our daughter, began speaking to me about veganism informing me she had taken the 30-day vegan pledge decisively stating "You are free to eat what you want, but I am not allowing any animal products in the house for the next 30-days." It was my decision or not to go vegan for 30-days with her. She had thrown down the vegan gauntlet.

It turns out our daughter Stephanie had been relaying her recent experience with going vegan for the past month. Years prior, unbeknownst to me, Stephanie had first tried a vegan 30-day pledge in college. She had been approached by an activist on the University of Michigan's campus and had signed up for email updates from vegsource, www.vegsource.com.  While her first vegan experience only lasted 30-days it spurred her to become an ova-lacto vegetarian for many years but when she moved to Italy she increasingly started to add meat back into her diet again. It was the vegsource emails that continued to come through her umich.edu account which had an educative effect on her. She learned about factory farming, the condition of egg laying hens and suffering of dairy cows. These emails and a Facebook connection to a vegan called Carrie, whose memes were very informative and thought provoking, led her to this latest 30-day challenge. Through the conversation, Stephanie had easily convinced her mother, who was in disbelief in learning about the plight of dairy cows and hen-laying chickens, to take the 30-day Vegan Pledge. Convinced by the graphic details provided by our daughter, Billie quickly linked health and ethical reasons for eating vegan and so I was greeted with a 30-day choice.

As an on and off again vegetarian I agreed to try it for 30-days. I really didn't have a big issue with 30-days of vegan eating but I distinctly remember telling her I was going to have a steak as soon as the 30-days were over. The last time I had been committed to vegetarianism was ten years earlier, and I had since fully recommitted myself to eating animal products. If there wasn't a slab of ribs, a burger, a sausage, a chicken breast or something completely smothered in cheese I wasn't feeling adequately nourished.

The dilemma for me was whether I could sit with the discomfort of no meat, fish, eggs or dairy for 30-days. With much bravado I had answered "yes" but it wasn't all that easy. It was a lot like meditation practice with physical leg, knee, and joint pains from sitting on the cushion, and mental pains from keeping your mind focused and refocused. I remember as I was going through the ordeal thinking it was only for 30-days and reminding myself to remember that I could put up with a little discomfort. It was certainly more compassionate, as a few less animals would end up slaughtered and so even if it was only for 30-days it was a good idea from that standpoint.

The first week was easy as I stuffed myself full of fruit, salad, pasta, bean tostadas with guacamole (Billie makes the best guacamole) and lentil soup with piping hot toast. The second week became difficult as cravings for animal products arose constantly no matter what I ate or how much. By the end of the third week cravings for beef, pork, chicken, and fish were for the most part subsided but the craving for dairy haunted me. This continued into and through the 4<sup>th</sup> week. For the most part my long term addiction and cravings were for cheese, except for one meat item that kept going through my head, beef steak. My wife, nevertheless, knew exactly how to deal with me by stating to me more than once: "OK, as soon as you can go out and kill a cow, skin it and butcher it yourself you can have one." Reality check, she hit me in the heart-of-compassion knowing I could never do that! I had always accepted that it was wrong to kill, wrong to hurt other sentient beings and every time I had ever done so I felt very remorseful. Throughout my life, the saying attributed to His Holiness the Dalai Lama has echoed in my head, "If you cannot help another, then at least do not harm them." This saying was always a compass pointing to true north. But here I was, wanting a big fat juicy steak as soon as this 30-day challenge was over and realizing an animal had to die to make this happen. Why was I not able to perform the act when I wanted someone else to do it for me?

   I opposed my cravings by combining meditation and research. One meditation technique I used was a very simple one, from beginning meditation 101, when one is taught to watch one's breath solely focusing on the breath with each in breath and out breath. In general when we do this we learn that our mind wanders so much that in classical texts it has been compared to a "wild elephant" as it will roam wherever it wants. The training tells you to simply bring the mind back gently to the breath each and every time you see it drifting. You may notice where it wandered, you accept it, you try to have no feelings for it, and then gently move your focus back to the breath. You can use gentle reminders to yourself to "be here now" and you sit, watching. What one notices is, if you simply sit with the feelings or thoughts without judgment and watch: they will pass. What arises passes. Everything changes and continues to change. Even our cravings are fleeting. And where did my mind go to during this time period? It told me I was hungry, it told me I needed meat, it told me I could have just one slice of cheese, it told me a couple pieces of pepperoni cheese pizza would taste so good, it reminded me of how a double-cheeseburger and fries were so tasty. I was tempted over and over again. But I just watched, dismissed and breathed. Sometimes I would offer alternative promptings to my mind:

- Are you really hungry?
- What does your stomach feel like?
- You just ate
- You don't need meat it's a proven fact
- You don't need massive amounts of protein

Gently I would tell myself no and go back to the breath. Each time I did this the cravings would have less and less of a grip. I watched my dairy cravings come and go. Sometimes they went quickly. Sometimes they went slowly. But after years of daily meditation practice I had become very used to watching my mind wander around and the whole addiction to food was interesting to observe and a real learning experience.

I first came to appreciate and practice meditation in my late teens. This was the early 1970s and 60's cultural influences were still very contemporary. Those of us listening were all exposed to the "turn on, turn in and drop out" message. My meditation teachers were authors and their books, and the experiences with psychedelics I explored. Aldous Huxley, Timothy Leary, A.C. Bhaktivedanta Swami Prabhupada, Suzuki, Mahareshi

Maresh Yogi, Lobsang Rampa, Tom Wolfe, Erich Fromm, Christmas Humphreys, Shri Guru Maharaj Ji, Carlos Castaneda, Lao Tzu, Chaung Tzu, J. Krishnamurti, and Alan Watts were authors whose books I read and they had a persuasive and compelling effect on my interest in meditation and Eastern spiritual thought. Additionally, the music of The Beatles, The Doors, and Jimi Hendrix all articulated messages which evoked inquisitiveness in this area. All these individuals influenced me and I read: The Bhagavad Gita, The Upanishads, The Vedas, Introduction to Zen, The Third Eye, The Teachings of Don Juan, The Electric Kool-Aid Acid Test, Cosmic Consciousness, The Doors of Perception, The Teachings of the Masters of the Far East, The Tao Te Ching, and The Book: On the Taboo Against Knowing Who You Are. I loved Alan Watts. I owned, and read, every single book Alan ever published and one of my favorite pastimes were Saturday night discussions with friends on the meaning of life, Eastern religion, and the books we were reading. Bringing in the Sunday dawn, these evenings were capped off with a 5:00 am Alan Watts recording on some Zen Buddhist teaching courtesy of WABX 99.5 FM, the local Detroit "progressive rock" station.

It was at this time I first tried meditation and I found my mind was unable to pause unless slumbering. I tried over and over without the success I anticipated. The mantras I had learned did not help. I didn't get it or have a teacher, my legs became numb, my mind wandered or I fell asleep, I couldn't focus and I eventually I put it on a shelf after a few years of on-and-off striving. Nonetheless, something had developed within me and somehow the effort gave me an appreciation and glimpse of something that resonated as true and would be of benefit. However, it wasn't until 1997 that I began a daily sitting practice again. This practice was now more formalized and based on studies in Tibetan Buddhism under the guidance and direction of Kyabje Gelek Rimpoche.[1]

I used meditation in parallel with education, which the Tsongkhapa Gelug Buddhist tradition puts a high value on, to combat my cravings. Learning is central to this Buddhist tradition because without knowledge what can we meditate upon? Consequently I started reading "The China Study" by T. Colin Campbell in which I learned that my habitual practices were unnecessary and even harmful to my health. Animal products had a negative effect on my health and a positive effect on the promotion of heart disease, diabetes, osteoporosis, some cancers, and more. I discovered I was habituated to eating things damaging for my body.

Eating unhealthily is against Buddhist tenets because the Buddha taught that you and your body are precious and should be taken care of. The first of the "Four Thoughts that Turn the Mind to the Dharma" details how this birth in a human lifeform is precious since we have the endowments, five inner and five outer, which afford us the ability to complete our task of awakening.[2] In brief, if we have found ourselves born as human in a country where the Dharma is taught and valued, and have the freedom, ability, time, food, warmth, safety, teachers and teachings we have been given a great opportunity to cultivate spiritual development. If we are endowed with the physical attributes to enable us to practice and learn, we have been given special ability. To enable learning we need good hearing, sight, and the ability to reason and think. Without these qualities practicing the Dharma becomes much harder. Therefore if we make ourselves sick we may not have the physical attributes to accomplish the path and will find ourselves suffering with the pain and misery of disease(s) and the powerful drug therapies used to treat them. Additionally, knowing this body and life is temporary and very ephemeral we should not prematurely hasten its end by eating food which stimulates illness.

So I watched my addictions and cravings arise, and then continued to dismiss them. Cravings arose, I accepted them, acknowledged them, felt them, proposed alternatives, and dismissed them time and time again. When they arose at times I reached for fruit, grains, veggies and vegan snacks. I ate as much as I wanted in that 30-day period, which helped with banishing cravings as much as the meditation. What was motivating was that after 30-days my cravings for beef, pork, chicken, fish, and eggs were gone -- completely eradicated! I had created a *new* habit, a *healthy* habit, a *compassionate* habit and I realized I had acquired something new in the vacuum of an animal based diet—taste buds for plant-based food. I realized I was tasting food in ways I never had in 55 years.

The story for dairy products, especially cheese, was a little different. In the absence of cheese usage I quickly realized I had used cheese on everything in the past. Cheese was the main dairy product I consumed as I had never been a milk drinker. I was still craving cheese after 30-days. I wanted Reggio Parmesan on my pasta, I wanted mozzarella cheese on pizza, and I wanted cheddar on my veggie burger. In short, I wanted to go back to my vegetarian roots, as there was something about dairy which was extremely addictive. Be that as it may, I did not and devoted myself to another 30-day vegan commitment. I was feeling great! I was eating as much as I wanted, and I was losing a little weight. Everything was good except for the little cheese monkey on my shoulder, that I kept watching and dismissing. It was during this second 30-day commitment that I started reading the book Eating Animals by Jonathan Safran Foer. This book informed me about factory farming and my eyes were fully opened to things I had never known nor wanted to know. An ignorant attraction to animal products was replaced by fully-aware repulsion. I began then and there to thank Dr. Campbell and Mr. Foer for forever changing my life. What I learned about dairy in Eating Animals and The China Study left indelible imprints on my mind, heart and spirit.

Shockingly, I found out that dairy is really a form of liquid meat and that the dairy industry is crueler to animals than the beef industry. I learned that the life of a dairy cow was about three and one-half years to five years of age. Additionally she has each of her calves taken from her at birth, which she mourns, lives in captivity the entire time, and eventually goes to slaughter just as all other farmed animals. Dairy can be called liquid meat because it has some of the same properties. It is high in cholesterol, protein, and fat and thus clogs arteries in the same fashion as other animal products. Furthermore, dairy, like meat, contains growth hormones and antibiotics, which are approved for use by the FDA. I was an addict, and cheese was my drug of choice due to the protein casein it contains. Casein breaks down in the stomach into various protein fragments one of which is: casomorphin. When we digest milk, yogurt, and cheese we break it down into casomorphin which has an opioid effect (think morphine, heroin, etc.) and we become dependent on this[3]. And yes, there is a withdrawal symptom from its elimination from the diet and an ever so slight euphoria we get by ingesting it. My dairy problem was related to the uncomfortable effects of very mild withdrawal. After 30-days on the vegan pledge with no cheese, I was still craving cheese. Perhaps this explains why it is so hard for some vegetarians to become vegan? If you've ever tried to kick the dairy habit you know what I am talking about.

Finally, I had found out why it was taking me so long to eliminate cravings for cheese when the other cravings had left. Casomorphin. I was addicted to a concentrated version of cow's milk, much stronger than the milk which a calf drinks. It takes 10 pounds of milk to make 1 pound of cheese, and I could easily down half of a pound of cheese or more on a pizza, or in cubes with crackers, or in the course of the day of three Standard-American-Diet meals (i.e. cheese on the omelet for breakfast, double-cheese on the burger for lunch, and macaroni and cheese with the dinner meal). I used to love cheese with anything. I loved the concentrated casein, fat, and the high levels of mother-cow-opiates I received from eating it. It was my inconsequential-form of legal opiates and I didn't even know it.

It took me a full six months to wipe out dairy cravings. But finally the cravings left and I lost thirty pounds around my waistline. I went from 222 lbs. to 192 lbs. without even trying. This, in and of itself, is amazing because I was eating as much or more food than when I was on the standard American diet. As plant-based whole-food is lower in fat, I was consuming less fat and as a consequence fat was being eliminated from my body. It's that simple. Plant-based whole-foods are lower in calories and higher in fiber and so I was feeling full but eating fewer calories.

Although it is a very simple formula, going vegan was, and is not, a cake walk. It means putting up with temporary pain and uneasiness. To a certain extent it means arguing with our own selves, with lots of self-talk and even dealing with emotions when they arise.

The longer I went without eating animal products the stronger I got and the less command the negative habits held. Foregoing animal products was worth the price of some temporary discomfort because it freed me from the bondage of eating cruelty and death. It freed me from my own suffering and watching my health decline early from standard western diseases that in many cases are reversible through diet.

Sitting there for 30-days with each and every meal, with every meditation practice session and with each book/blog or article I read, was not easy. It brought up issues with my ego, my family traditions, my comfort with friends and sangha members and not fitting in, accompanied by my need to be liked. I didn't fit in the world the same way. I couldn't find things to eat at work or at restaurants. The cafeteria at work didn't serve one vegan item but iceberg lettuce with oil and vinegar, not to mention Thanksgiving turkey and annual family trips to Frankenmuth for "All-You-Can-Eat family style chicken dinner". But I needed to persevere as the alternative was going to be heart disease and diabetes for me and long list of escalating medications for the rest of my life accompanied by the requisite side effects. Not to mention potential hospitalizations and surgeries and thousands animals who were going to be bred into captivity and slaughtered on my behalf.

So going vegan has been a lot like meditating on my neuroses, accepting myself, loving myself, sitting with myself, forgiving myself and changing myself with each and every day and getting further from the discomfort. Each day that I sat with my feelings of discomfort it became a little easier (like quitting smoking). The feelings of discomfort didn't go away easily, but I learned I could handle the addictions and habits and I didn't need to feed them. The whole need, want and desire was dissipating as I watched it. Just like watching my breath and bringing my mind back into focus, I was ridding my body, mind, and spirit of the fear of the loss of meat, fish, dairy and eggs.

I was becoming more in control of my choices for food. While learning to choose compassion over killing, my body was reaping the benefits and my mind asked for more knowledge, more understanding and more commitment. Soaking in every book I could get my hands on, I read nonstop. I gave into my change, fully immersed and saturated myself with discussions on Facebook, blog readings, and library loans. As my mind assimilated the brain material and brushed away cravings, my physical body also changed from the plant-based whole-food I was feeding it. My hydration levels improved due to the high water content of the foods I was eating. I was releasing toxins and creating a physical foundation for spiritual and energetic changes to occur. As energy improved, healing was occurring; I was flooding myself with minerals, vitamins and thousands of antioxidants from natural sources. Everything was easily absorbed into my system and my bloodstream, glands, organs, lymph nodes, brain, liver, kidneys, and every tissue was being gently cleansed with the true elements necessary for a healthy life. My hormones were working better, the naturally occurring steroids my body produces were working better, and all my neurotransmitters were firing in a more healthful, vibrant and energetic way. My diet had allowed my body to return to homeostasis. The debris of eating misery, pain, and death was breaking up and leaving my body. I was moving easier, was in less arthritic-like pain, was losing weight, and the chemical results from lab tests proved it.

At the end of 30-days most cravings had disappeared and after 6 months I was hooked to a new lifestyle and concurrently I had learned a great lesson about changing habitual patterns. I had faced my habitual patterns, sat with them, and learned I was stronger than my obsessions, habits and meat attachment. I had discovered that the addictions would go away, that nothing tastes as good as health feels, and that nothing tastes as good as love feels. I was truly more in love with all of life. I was no longer responsible for sentient beings being enslaved on factory farms, paying someone to kill them for me, and their murder in slaughterhouses. I had learned that nothing tastes as good as compassion feels and ultimately living my life more in line with the teachings from the Buddha, freed from the attachment to animal products, and most importantly, I was living in line with my own moral intelligence.

## Watch the Craving

"Watch the craving", much like a meditation practice, is a tactic I have employed for working through cravings for meat, fish, dairy and eggs. Bring your mind to bear on this feeling, this craving. Feel it fully become aware of it, concentrate on it, the feeling you have, the taste you crave, the body's sensations, the thought of it, sit with it for a moment, acknowledge it, and then gently release it. Do not try to push it away too quickly, deny it, or use anything negative, or angry to deal with it. Realize it's just a habit, an attachment, a craving, it's nothing to label, it's not you, it's not negative, it's not positive, it just is. Watch it. Then you'll notice it will start to dissipate, it will loosen its grip, when it begins to loosen, release it and move on. This is how I have dealt with these feelings of eating meat. It's a practice of meditation without sitting on a cushion. It's watching your mind during everyday life and can be used in any situation. It's a way to gently deal with something you want to change in your mind. Changing your mind will also in this case help your body and contribute to your awakening more compassion. When we make an incremental change in the way we eat, we change how we look at ourselves; we change in the way we look at other sentient beings, the way we look at our resources on the planet, and the people who desperately need those resources.

Change takes courage. When I kept coming back to acknowledge my cravings for meat, my cravings didn't instantly go away. I had to remember I was trying to change something that was deeply ingrained, like an oil stain in cloth, my lifetime of eating meat. Eating animals is deeply ingrained for most of us, it is ingrained in our society, and wherever we go we are confronted with eating meat. Changing our eating habits is very much a meditation practice; it is very much like Alcoholics Anonymous 12 steps, or anything else you wish to change. However, becoming vegan is very doable because you are substituting meat, fish, dairy and eggs with healthy, delicious food with so many alternative choices. Vegan food has never tasted so good and been so available. Nothing can keep its hooks in you when you do not engage it and when you fully change your diet to a vegan diet the lure of meat, eggs, dairy and cheese and fish will dissipate like morning fog. The cravings, habitual addictions, your need, the feel of your need, the belief that you have to have meat to be healthy -- will go away and you become more wholesome.

## The Buddha and Angulimala: We Can All Change

It is a foggy mist laden dawn heavy with expectancy. The killer slowly creeps up behind another tree making up the space between himself and his next victim, his last quarry. Momentarily hidden quietly behind the tree and tall grass he peeks out. The robed man is still not any closer. Anger consumes Angulimala. His face reddens and he looks for another tree but there isn't one. Gasping for one last breath he decides to just make a run for his last victim, knife in hand he begins to inaudibly run, gathering speed, he is coming closer to his unwary victim. "Good the victim is too absorbed and hasn't perceived me." Just a little closer. Running harder, he tries to make the final 25 feet but cannot. With every step he makes the slow walking man is just that much further. He is really mad now and yells to the victim "STOP!" The victim doesn't reply but just keeps walking at his normal speed, absorbed, head slightly down, peaceful and tranquil. Angulimala tries once more to close the distance but cannot continue. His heart feels like it is going to pound out of his chest. He stops and lays sprawled on the tall wet grass, with hawk eyes still on his elusive prey. The man in the robe stops and turns looking deeply into Angulimala's eyes and just rests in the gaze--concerned and undaunted. Angulimala is almost rested now enough to try again, he will get his victim, he will get the elusive man, this man who challenges him so, stopping and looking at me will be his downfall, stupid man.

Angulimala is up and running again, eyes transfixed on his victim in a completely animalistic mind, nothing exists, nothing else is present, no tree, no grass, no person, no knife, no pain, no lack of pain, no person, just him and his victim, it seems like he has been running now for minutes and hours, time stops, he realizes he is crying, he realizes he is not getting any closer nor further, he realizes he cannot do what he set out to do, he realizes there is no need for him to do what wanted to do, he realizes the pain and suffering he has caused his victims and their families, sees all their faces, and he realizes that this man his last victim he will not kill, cannot kill, but can only love. The man has only love. The man has only compassion. What has happened to me? Why am I crying? Why am I feeling this way? What has come over me? I am so tired of fighting. I will stop.

At that moment he catches the Buddha. Knife still in hand he sits on the ground. Bewildered and yet clear, he drops the knife and prostrates to the Buddha. "Master," he says, "please forgive me, I wished to become enlightened and make a gift to my former master and would have killed you. You were the last victim I needed. But I could not and I do not know why. Please help me."

The Buddha walks up to Angulimala and touches his face. Never dropping his gaze with the killer and Angulimala hears, "Be at peace my son. Know that you have all you need to become awake. Be at peace. Be in this moment. Rest. No harm will befall you. I love you."
At once Angulimala is transfixed. Never has one even spoken the words, "I love you" and although he didn't see the mouth of the man move he clearly heard all the words. "Please let me be your student. I denounce my

former master. I will never kill again. Please kind Guru let me be your student."

The Buddha spoke this time, "Yes, you can be my student." With that the Buddha turned and went back to walking the promenade around the Gandakuti temple seemingly vanishing in the contemplative mist still fully absorbed in deep meditation.

The magical place where this historical story is set and originated is called "The Jetavana Grove". It is in the outskirts of the city of Sravasti in the state of Bihar, one of the few places where the Buddha is said to have performed many miracles. The Jetavana Grove is a place of wonder and rich history where the Buddha spent the monsoon season for 20 years. He and his followers watched the torrents come down and sat practicing.

Sitting today my mind wanders over historical story of Angulimala, the killer of 999 people in India during the Buddha's time who had a previous master that told him if he killed one thousand people and brought back the evidence he would be liberated. Angulimala, as the story goes went around killing all the people he could in order to make his one thousand count. He was obviously feared and thus shunned by city dwellers and villagers alike who stayed away from him not wanting to be one of his victims. Angulimala means "Finger Rosary" and he got this name because after each killing, he would cut a finger from the victim and string it onto a necklace which he wore. So the story goes that he was at 999 fingers when he sort of got stuck and could not find victim number 1,000. Reviled and dreaded having a reputation that went far and wide he was having trouble getting his last victim. The only person who was not completely afraid of him was his mother and he could not find it within himself to kill his own mother. Luckily for him the

Buddha was walking nearby and Angulimala believed he had found his last victim. The story goes that each and every time Angulimala tried to catch up to, ambush, flank and capture the Buddha he failed. This all the while the Buddha was just strolling along casually while Angulimala was running frantically to try and catch up. Finally in desperation Angulimala yells out to the Buddha and tells him to stop, which the Buddha does and a dialogue ensues. The conversation leads to Angulimala realizing he had been lied to by his teacher, that even if he killed another person to get his 1000th kill he would not be liberated. And so he became a student of the Buddha then and there. Legend tells us Angulimala became enlightened, never killed again, following the way of the Buddha, supporting people and all sentient beings in whatever way he could. He was of course never trusted by anyone including former family and friends from the city. To the family and friends of those he had murdered he was hated, reviled and insulted all the rest of his life but he never retaliated and humbly took whatever was given him, good and bad.

So what kind of a story is this? What does it speak to? If we suspend judgment and accept this story as having some essence of truth it becomes a classic story of someone doing something morally wrong and acting in a way that creates abundant negativity, bad karma and a pathway to a negative rebirth. It is also about a person who finds a way to change and is able to refocus his life. Imagine the drive Angulimala must have had to pursue the life of a killer, alone, dreaded, living on the outskirts of civilization waiting for victims. Imagine how convinced he must have been, how attached and used to killing he must have become after so many deaths. Imagine how skilled at his "craft" he was and the injuries he must have experienced over the years with victims who fought back and the men who banded together to hunt him down and kill him. He was on the wrong path but thinking he was on the right path.

How different was he than you and I? Not very different. I reflect on the concept I first read by the late Norm Phelps in his book <u>The Great Compassion</u> that we are all like Angulimala collecting our rosary of fingers by eating animals every day. We go around acting like its normal, like there is nothing wrong with it. During a life of eating meat I myself collected enough "fingers", paws, claws, feet, hands and wings to create a mala of more than 5,000 beads long. My personal rosary of death was very long because for the first 55 years of my life I ate a lot of meat, fish, dairy and eggs.

Like Angulimala, I finally realized that what I was doing was somehow not right. I was slowly getting sick with standard American "western" disease, even though I worked out every day. I was overweight. My blood pressure and sugar levels were too high. My meditation practice was feeling stagnated and I didn't feel like I was making progress along the spiritual path. I was swimming laps in the pool of life and no matter how hard I swam I could not catch up to the Buddha. He was always one flip turn ahead of me, one meditation, one set of yoga poses, one book, one retreat, and one enlightening conversation away, flip. I was just like Angulimala, stuck in a negative activity. I was the cause of killing of beings whom I was praying to be liberated each day. My meditation practices informed me of the opposite. The teachings informed me of the opposite. My heart informed me of the opposite. Logic and analysis informed me of the opposite. But habit, taste, ease, and denial were my true friends, the one's I listened to, so much like Angulimala's "evil" teacher. I didn't take time really listen to the true teacher within, my own Buddha nature.

One day, however, just like Angulimala, I woke up but it was not until I had made a commitment to not put "fingers" onto my rosary for a month that this occurred (30-day vegan pledge). The 30-day commitment allowed me some space to open up and gave me the impetus to learn more. It allowed my ego to pause. I began to do research. I analyzed what "we" as a society were doing and what I was doing as a person and whether or not what I was doing actually aligned with my moral code, my ethics of living, and my spiritual path. I found my behavior lacking and so I changed.

The 30-day experiment has turned into more than 5 years and a commitment for the rest of my life. I will not eat the bodies, eggs or excretions (milk, or liquid meat) or wear the remnants of a corpse (leather, fur) ever again. I have stopped putting fingers on my personal rosary and this has had a clearing effect for my head and conscience. It has helped me to live a kind, more compassionate and loving life.

As such this path aligns with the path of the Bodhisattva; it helps us become more centered, grounded and open to a more honest form of mindfulness. At a minimum we become grounded at each and every meal because we can look at our plate with full acknowledgment that no one has died and suffered to become a meal for our body. We can become like Angulimala listening to the compassionate Buddha within and changing. And that can become a lesson for others. We can all change if we choose to do so. We can all become healthier in our bodies, mind, and spirit by becoming more compassionate with our eating. We can all have a smaller carbon footprint immediately and help our Earth Mother. We can help eliminate the death of approximately 200 food animals per year and an incalculable number of by-catch sea creatures.

Just like Angulimala each one of us can change and become compassionate. That is the true story of Angulimala. If a killer of 999 people can change we can too. And if we look close enough we are not different and even if you are a killer you can change what you are doing and become a Buddha, whose heart is ultimate love and compassion for all sentient beings.[4]

# Health Effects

What really made me feel good from a health standpoint was my first visit to my doctor for my annual physical. Here is the council I received from my doctor five years prior to becoming vegan (see if any of this resonates with you or one of your loved ones):

1. John, you need to lose weight. Try working out more and eating more fruits and vegetables. The extra weight you are carrying is not good for your health.
2. John, your blood pressure is borderline high; we really need to watch that. If it gets any higher we really need to put you on some blood pressure medicine. High blood pressure is a risk factor for many diseases.
3. John, your sugar level is borderline high, we really need to watch this as I know diabetes runs in your family. Diabetes is a terrible disease, which left untreated, can cause many other terrible side effects.

4. John, your cholesterol is too high we need to keep you on the statin drug we have you on. Even on that drug you're borderline high. We may need to increase it.
5. John, your triglycerides are off the charts, let's switch you from Lipitor to Tricor which has a better effect on high triglycerides. Keep taking these every day as you are a candidate for a heart attack or stroke with these levels. The drugs can help keep the high levels in check.

After six months on a 100% vegan diet and losing 25 lbs. here's how my first annual physical went:

> Doctor: John, what did you do to lose all this weight?
>
> John: I went vegan.
>
> Doctor: Good for you. That is probably one of the best things you've ever done in your life. Your blood pressure is completely normal and I would imagine your sugar, cholesterol and triglyceride levels are lower too, let's see how your lab results come out.
>
> John: Thanks, Doctor. Why didn't you tell me about a vegan diet before if it's a good thing to do?
>
> Doctor: Eating more fruits and vegetables are always a good thing to do but most people will not change their diet so drastically, so as doctors we just do not bring it up.

So, how did the labs turn out?

- Sugar levels: normal

- Cholesterol levels: "low" normal
- Triglycerides level: normal

I called my doctor and we discussed me quitting all statin drugs. He agreed we could try this as I was staying on a vegan diet. He stressed we needed to continue to monitor the lab results and maybe run a lipids (cholesterol/triglycerides) test within a few months to check my status without being on Tricor. I agreed and stopped taking the Tricor immediately.

Three months later I went back in to for a blood test and the results came back normal. My levels had not changed and I was not on any medication and getting great results from being on a vegan diet.

Five years later all my lab work is still at normal levels. My cholesterol is 155 mg/dL. My weight fluctuates based on my love for bread, pasta, olive oil and other processed foods. But I have never put back on the weight I was carrying when I was eating a standard American diet. I am down from a 36 inch waist to a 34 inch waist and when my clothes get a little tight I simply cut processed foods and stick with only whole foods. By simply eating whole foods my calorie consumption goes down and weight naturally starts coming off. I know I should only eat whole foods but that effort is still a work in progress.


# Discarding Cultural Baggage

What began to unfold in my mind stream after going vegan for a few months was a complete metamorphosis of my thought patterns, beliefs and perspective on what is nutritious to eat and what is not. I began to discard the old cultural thoughts just as I had discarded the habits. I can remember my loving Calabrian grandmother telling me I needed to eat meat every once in a while, a big beef steak, or beef liver or my blood would not be healthy. I can remember ironically she would cook this for my loving aunt who died of cancer when I was just a boy.

My world of eating was being turned on its head. No more meatballs with pasta, now it was veggie "meat" balls with pasta, no more barbequed chicken now it was seared tofu with wonderful seasonings and colorful veggies on the side, no more bacon and eggs now it was faux bacon tempeh and tofu scramble. A whole new dietary world was opening up to me and in the space of 30-days something miraculous had happened—my tastes changed! I believe I was now tasting foods for the first time unmasked and completely without judging them on their lack of rich fat content. Food tasted good without animal fat, namely butter and cheese. I didn't need the drippings from meat to flavor things; I didn't need the high fat flavor of cheese or butter to enrich the flavor of natural good food. I used to be a complete snob when it came to vegan food; if a dish didn't have an animal product on the plate it wasn't a meal. Now I was truly enjoying food without it.

The other change that had occurred was my awareness/compassion meter had made a marked improvement. I was seeing things more realistically, more as they are in reality without denial, without setting aside feelings, without repression. I was allowing myself to feel, see, and make connections that I had not been able to make before because the cognitive dissonance had been so strong. I began to see what I had been eating was part of a cruel industry, a culture that commodifies animals, sentient beings who I was praying to save everyday as part of my Buddhist practice and meditations. Every sadhana (Sanskrit for practice) in the Tibetan Buddhist tradition begins and ends with the vow to free all sentient beings from suffering, to free them, to help them and to save them.

While I vowed to do this as a "Bodhisattva": declared to be reborn life-after-life to free all beings, until each and every one of them had achieved full and total enlightenment on one hand, with the other hand I was eating their lifeless cooked corpses and bodily secretions with my fork, knife and spoon. I now saw this plainly for the first time; my actions at almost every meal were in direct opposition to what I believed I was standing for. I thought I was standing for love and compassion but my love and compassion was only extended as far as me and other humans. I believed I was helping to slow global warming by purchasing cars which were not gas guzzlers, by recycling and donating to environmental causes but I was not. In each meal I was hurting sentient beings, causing more death via the marketplace and helping to create more global warming not less. I became very angry for a time. I was angry at myself for not seeing it and angry with Buddhist leaders who were as silent on these issues as our society is in general. I was seeing this issue as a clear cut example of abysmal structural violence. It was a shallow bitter time for me. I felt betrayed by my teachers, by the books they wrote and the talks they gave. In short, I felt deceived and let down. Fortunately, it was short lived.

# The Mindful Vegan and the Holiday Dinner

*"Our awareness of feelings in the body and mind ranges from simple frustration and malaise to anguish, despair, and white-hot physical pain, and from simple pleasures to extraordinary ecstasy. As we become clearly cognizant of the bandwidth of our own feelings, we direct our awareness externally. We become vividly aware that myriad sentient beings around us are not simply objects of our pleasure, displeasure, or indifference, but have feelings just like ours. By turning our awareness outward and closely applying mindfulness to other sentient beings, we can empathize with their feelings. When we empathize with another's suffering and we attend closely, compassion arises. The suffering of unpleasant feelings is the very source of the experience of compassion."*
B. Alan Wallace; MINDING CLOSELY: THE FOUR APPLICATIONS OF MINDFULNESS[5]

Our family met last year at a generic chain Italian restaurant across from a mall as we have done for the past three years. It's centrally located and gives us all a chance to get together for a meal prior to my parents going to Florida for the winter months. The restaurant is not fine dining by any measure but it's not fast food either. As a restaurant that has its roots in Italian cooking it does offer some vegan options. So, thirteen of us got together and had a "nice" meal, some conversation and exchanged pleasantries. From the point of view of us getting together I like the occasion; from the point of view of the meal it serves as a typical example of what a mindful vegan experiences.

The server came around and asked for drinks and then brought salads and bread sticks. All you can eat salad and bread sticks are provided by restaurant, it's part of their business model. As a vegan I have learned what and what not to ask for over the years. Their standard salad comes with parmesan cheese grated over the top, Italian house dressing with cheese in it, and the bread sticks come hot out of the oven slathered with butter. Billie and I ordered a salad with no cheese, no dressing, with olive oil and vinegar on the side and bread sticks with no butter. Three salads come out to the table, two of them "normal" salads with loads of cheese and house dressing along with four servings of bread sticks. We all started serving ourselves. As a vegan, the smell of cheese now smells like death and I must sit and watch as my sister, nephew, mom and dad and cousins all partake in the salads drenched in cheese. What I see is not a pleasant sight. It comes in fractions of a second and I force it out and move on knowing I cannot do anything about it. Visions of cows hooked up to sucking tubes come into my head, workers beating them to make them comply scroll by, in the visual cortex of my brain, cattle prods, angry shouts, and abusive confinement on concrete floors are all there too. I witness baby calves in the wonderful splendor of birth, wet, making sounds of helplessness, looking for their mother and the mother licking them giving them one feeding from the milk of her body. I next hear the bellowing heart wrenching sound of the baby being taken from her mother. Both calf and mother crying out, crying out, crying out. Helpless with no relief for their pain. The cheese on the fork of a family member with salad dressing dripping from the lettuce cries to me from across the table. I look away but another family member is talking about going to see a popular movie just out in theaters, while he holds a bread stick dripping with butter, I am transported again. This time I am witnessing a pen, a small little house and the baby calf, a male calf who is still crying for its mother. He is wobbly and weak. He has very little room to move. There is a bottle hanging from the fence with some white liquid in it, he is tasting it and drinking it but it's not his mother's milk, it's a substitute formula where much of the nutrition he needs to grow strong and healthy is missing. He is not destined to live long, because "we" do not want him to become strong as his meat will become too tough for the veal market.

Back at the meal we are finishing our first course and the main dishes are starting to appear. Across the table one family member has ordered a vegan meal just like Billie, capellini with Pomodoro sauce, but she had opted for the added shrimp when it was suggested by the server. Seeing it served I am whisked away to South East Asia. I am hearing Vietnamese being spoken and am in a small boat examining the crop of shrimp growing in a former Mangrove field where no Mangrove's exist today. I hear the pumps running, a slight drone in the background as machines provide aeration and flushing needed to keep the crop alive. In front of me is a dense pond filled with thousands of sentient beings, little shrimp, all trying to escape into the ocean. It's a filthy disgusting pond, riddled with pesticides and antibiotics, non-organic fertilizer, commercial feed and pig feces. The poor creatures are bacteria and virus laden, packed so densely they can hardly breathe while above I see an algae bloom that spreads as far as my eye can see polluting and killing off all other sentient beings in area not equipped with the additional aeration provided by the pumps and motors running onshore. Flies buzz around the large mound of pig excrement on the shore in this intensive production scene in one of the poorest nations on earth, hopeful sweat saturated brows wipe the salty sweat away, eyeing the prize of thousands of writhing struggling beings with dollar signs in their gaze, hoping to care for their families and become rich.[6] Back at the dinner another family member has just been served pasta with pork sausage and I just turn into my own plate as the vision of pigs in suffering in factory confinement enters my mind. I take a bite of my pizza with tomato sauce, olives, mushrooms, onions, green pepper and no cheese. I rest mindfully on my plate without suffering and I am thankful no sentient beings died for my meal.

## Shallow Veganism: The Anger Stage

After 30-days I began to see dairy in a much different light. I saw it as a cruel practice that enslaved mothers, kidnapped babies, murdered male offspring (veal) and finally murdered the "spent" cows (cows whose milk production had fallen below accepted levels of productivity) who were sent to slaughter. I began to make the connections between what I had been eating and what it was doing to the animals, the planet and my health. Dairy was liquid meat. It was no different that eating beef, chicken, pork or fish. Perhaps in some aspects it was crueler because it enslaved its participants, made them suffer for years, made them anguish for days each time their baby was taken from them and finally sent them to the same slaughterhouse as the rest. Cheese became a baby's stolen milk, a mother's grief, suffering legs, hoofs, and mastitis each and every time I saw it and see it today.

I had uncovered the truth so I thought others would want to know. I spoke about this to others, beginning to inform where I could, doing "vegan outreach" by teaching others about the issues, sharing books, sharing blogs and sharing articles. I was amazed to find out many people didn't want to know the truth, didn't want to hear it, discuss it, or have me even suggest it. This was disconcerting for me when it came to many of my spiritual community, "sangha" members, people I have known and loved for many years. I have seen them at numerous retreats and we have spent many hours discussing dharma topics, debating, sharing, and caring for one another. To find out they did not want to hear about this truth I had just uncovered for myself was a big disappointment. To have them block me on Facebook was a revelation of how deep the cognitive dissonance ran in our culture and within our spiritual community.

In the first few months of going vegan remarkable things had happened to me, my health had improved, my ability to be more open to learn new things had improved, and I was eating with more compassion and had lowered my carbon footprint in the process. There had been a body, mind and spirit change, a compassionate upheaval. However, becoming an outsider in my spiritual community was not one of the changes I had anticipated. No one really wanted to hear about this and this made me angrier. I unknowingly entered the first stage of veganism, the anger stage.

# "Yeah, But"

During this initial vegan stage of anger I really had a strong disdain for "Yeah, Buts". They really made the hair on my back rise. What's a "Yeah, But"? Picture yourself having an intelligent conversation with a long term Buddhist practitioner, a person devoted to looking inward and changing themselves, and they say to you in agreement "Yeah, but I could never give up _____" (insert your favorite animal product). The particular "yeah, but" I have heard most often is around cheese, "Yeah, but I could never give up cheese" is the single most used "yeah, but" that I have heard during earnest conversations about going vegan. Most people agree that harming animals is morally wrong, Buddhist's take vows to not harm, however when it comes to giving something up that we have a strong attachment to, we ignore the moral feelings and the vows. I know my cravings and desire for cheese continued for six-months very strongly. Yet, I kept telling myself no, it was wrong to support an industry that takes a mother's baby away after birth and keeps her confined, drugged, continually pregnant, and suffering for her entire short life. I would visualize suffering mothers doing a quick analytical meditation, each and every time the craving became strong. It took a long time but I retrained my brain. I took control. I exercised discipline and used meditation. If I could see this and do this, why was I getting all these "yeah but" responses?

I had my own "yeah buts" now. Yeah, but isn't this what the Buddha did? Yeah, but didn't he change his mind to become totally compassionate? Yeah, but isn't this what any Bodhisattva would do? Yeah, but wasn't Atisha, Milarepa, Khendrup Je, Shabkar and others vegetarian lamas in old Tibet? Yeah, but you can use Tofu, soy milk, almond milk and hemp milk. Yeah, but you can use "Beyond Meat Chicken", Daiya cheese, Lite Life bacon, Tofurky Tempeh bacon, Veganaise, and various egg replacers. Yeah, but you can change your tastes. Yeah, but you could do a 30-day vegetarian pledge and then do a 30-day vegan pledge (baby steps). Yeah, but you can be more compassionate.

In the first stage of veganism I was angry and I apologize to anyone I hurt during the process. At times I had become what I disliked so much a, "Yeah, but".

Between anger and "Yeah, but" there is a middle ground where we stand ready to strongly fight for the welfare of all sentient beings and do so without judgment and anger. We live, speak and embody the truth without attachment to it.

When I think about Atisha (980 AD), Milarepa (1052), Khendrup Je (1385), Shabkar (1781), and Patrul Rinpoche (1808) living in Tibet at the time they did and being vegetarian, I cannot begin to imagine how difficult it was.[7] But they somehow kept their commitments and vows. They didn't have substitutes for meat like we do (nor was there a dairy industry like today that functions by treating animals inhumanely). We have so many choices today. We have alternatives for meat, for dairy and for eggs. I have not run across a recipe I loved that could not be veganized.[8] If it can be veganized then why would a Buddhist practitioner choose cruelty over kindness? For me it was just culture, habit and taste. Just as there is no reason for anger, there is no reason to be a "Yeah, but" because it's just working with your mind and changing it.

# Analytical Meditation and Changing Your Habits

There are many types of meditation in the Buddhism, samatha (tranquility), vipassana (insight), anapanasati (breathing), metta (loving kindness), karmasthana (place of work), mahasati (dynamic), zazen (seated), koan (breakthrough), tonglen (giving and receiving), mahamudra (great seal), dzogchen (great perfection), phowa (transference), four immeasurables (loving kindness), analytical (reasoning and logic), concentrated (focusing or resting) and the list goes on and on. All are related. All have the same goal to create tranquil abiding in the mind leading to more stability, clarity, understanding, compassion and wisdom. Some are so similar it is only cultural form and language which separate them.

The two types of meditation I am most familiar with are analytical and concentrated from the Tibetan tradition. Analytical meditation is based upon study, reflection, and logical inquiry. It is founded on reasons, arguments, and conclusions.[9] This meditation form, as do all forms of meditation, takes effort! We must push ourselves to apply a logical sequence of points on a subject until the application of effort becomes effortless. This can and will occur in a very short time if you, with gentle force, apply and reapply yourself to this method. There will be benefits such as: increased awareness, deeper realization, and planting of seeds within your mind which will grow over time. Generally this type of meditation is used for developing a better understanding of impermanence and death, karma and its effects, emptiness and the stages of the path, Lam Rim.[10] What I propose, and have used, is a non-standard and uncommon approach to analytical meditation which has worked for me. I have used this meditation style to familiarize and remind myself of a new way of thinking about food. Sometimes I use it to zero in on a certain food.

The other type of meditation is concentrated meditation. It's also known commonly as single pointed meditation, resting meditation, and/or Samadhi when perfected. It is utilized when one has analyzed a situation, internal trait, negativity, virtue or something wishing to be changed and/or deepened within. When you come to a conclusion in analytical meditation, you use concentrated meditation to steep yourself in the hypothesis, like a tea bag in a cup of hot water, merging with it, sitting with it fully absorbed by it, with as much single-pointed concentration as you can muster. The two types work hand-in-hand when you are trying to change your mind, improve yourself, and make a change stick. Change is difficult and in Tibetan Buddhism these two types of meditation are deemed as necessary to break through ignorance and make a difference in our habitual behaviors.

Gelek Rimpoche states quite clearly, in the Three Principles of the Path:

> *"Analytical meditation is a must! Because the root of all problems lies in ignorance. Ignorance cannot be cleared by concentrated meditation alone. No! Concentrated meditation can reduce anger, concentrated meditation can reduce attachment, concentrated meditation is*

*tremendously helpful for emotional problems, but concentrated meditation cannot clear ignorance. In order to clear ignorance you need wisdom, and wisdom is only possible through analytical meditation."*[11]

While I used both of these types of meditation often during the first six-months of going vegan it was analytical meditation which made an indelible impact on me. It has, and continues to be, something I turn to when I am tempted by animal foods, when I am feeling my former habitualized cravings skulk back into my mind. When this occurs I utilize analytical meditation. In my mind I talk myself through the basic knowledge and logic of why it is I choose not to use or eat a particular animal product. I use the reasoning of this type of meditation to bring my mind back to a truer reality, which for me doesn't happen automatically because my natural state is one of confusion, attachment, and habit. We all long for what is comfortable even when it is not beneficial for us. I may know an animal product is not favorable for me but that does not necessarily translate into an antidote for the feeling I need to eat it.

Many of us are in the same boat. We are confused. We like what we are used to. We don't want to change or be "present" in the truth of eating meat, fish, dairy and eggs. I have had to walk myself through the logic of why meat eating is destructive, what exactly it is, reminding myself exactly where eggs come from, exactly where sausage comes from, exactly where a piece of cheese comes from, and exactly what kind of suffering is embodied within it—for both myself and for the being that gave its life. Examining why I feel I need it, when so many others who are vegan do not need this food, is sobering. Reminding myself how it can be toxic to my body, can lead toward disease states and how this has been overwhelmingly shown over and over again by scientific research--wakes me back up.

So for me becoming a vegan has grown into a Dharma practice to talk myself through both the physical and mental attributes of this lifelong attachment. As I did this, and do this, I am able to dissipate the cravings, need and routine. Habituating oneself in the experience of analytical meditation followed by a short concentrated meditation eventually becomes so instinctively easy you can effortlessly go through it and avoid the animal product. It has the ability to change your awareness and your entire mind on any subject you decide to point it towards.

Lama Je Tsongkhapa in the Lam Rim Chen Mo, the stages of the path to enlightenment, informs us that this type of meditation is necessary to familiarize ourselves with a different way of thinking,

> *"Analytical meditation is necessary for meditations such as those on faith in the teacher; the great importance and difficulty in obtaining leisure and opportunity; death and impermanence; karma and its effects; the faults of cyclic existence; and the spirit of enlightenment. This is because these meditations need an awareness that is long lasting, very forceful, and capable of changing the mind. Without this, you will not be able to stop the forces that oppose these meditations..."[12]*

Therefore, analytical meditation is a logical rationally-based influential approach to meditation. It is not blind faith but it's opposite and similar to the scientific inquiry on a personal level where you convince yourself, create a deeper understanding about something, or even gently remind yourself of something known to be true using reason.

An example of analytical meditation upon being confronted with the wish to eat fish or some seafood could go like this: Fish are sentient beings, they live in communities of other fish and can identify their relatives in schools of thousands, they feel pleasure and pain, they wish to be free in the ocean and have pleasurable experiences, this piece of a cod/salmon/crab/tuna in front of me or on this menu was such a being, she had rights and feelings, she wanted to live but was captured, dragged for miles/hours and then brought to the surface, she struggled with all her strength to escape, she gasped for air in the unfamiliar toxic atmosphere, she flipped and flopped in desperation on the ship's deck but was thrown on ice amid hundreds and perhaps thousands of others from her family and circle, all the others were also in pain, after hours of crushing pressure and cold temperature unable to move she slowly died unable to free herself, all the hormones and adrenaline of terror from the fight and life-ending struggle were released into her body during the capture and death process, and now I sit on the precipice of a decision, craving her body as food knowing full well if I order her or purchase her another being will be killed on my behalf. Is this what I want? Do I expect satisfaction from this meal? Can I expect to get nutrition or disease by bringing the corpse of this suffering being into my body? I have read all the literature and understand how many toxins there are in fish, mercury,

PCBs, and Dioxin, just to name a few. I know of the potential negative effects animal protein has on my body when ingested. I obviously do not want to eat this being, I have empathy and compassion for her, I have empathy and compassion for all cod/salmon/crab/tuna as I have empathy for all sentient life, I know bringing this being's body into my body will cause only more death and destruction. It will probably give me health problems; it will cause the market to continue because of my action, it will cause more damage to the planet and ocean in the form of more cod/salmon/crab/tuna being captured, more bycatch in the form of endangered sea turtles, and inquisitive playful dolphins. It will support the creation of more fish farms. I do not want sickness and pain. I do not want fish and bycatch to be caught, suffer and die miserably for my habits. I do not want the earth poisoned further on my behalf. I choose not to order or eat this cod/salmon/crab/tuna.

Next I switch to a short concentrated meditation session. I notice any feelings aroused by the analytical meditation. What is the feeling? How am I feeling mentally, emotionally and physically? Where is the feeling located? I look without judgement as I sit in gentle meditative focus, firm and yet relaxed on the resolution I have made. This can be done sitting, standing, alone, or in a group and by putting forth a little effort, just taking a couple minutes, I have found I no longer crave the fish. Each and every time we cycle through a situation like this we make a step forward in forever changing our tastes, habits and historical food patterns. We eventually become more conscious and wiser in our food choices. The masters teach that a simple meditation practice like this has the power to alter your cultural upbringing and bring about a complete metamorphosis in you wherever you point it at, whatever the trouble you are having, and wherever a change is needed.

As Gelek Rimpoche states,

*"Analytical meditation is the real weapon. Concentrated meditation is... stable and unshakeable. The real weapon however is wisdom. And without analytical meditation wisdom doesn't grow. Wisdom is not a mushroom that pops up. When you have some kind of half-rain, half fog on a high mountain overnight, the next morning you see mushrooms popping up. Wisdom doesn't grow that way; not at all. Nor does wisdom develop if you keep on sitting and waiting. Just closing your eyes and thinking that everything is pure and wonderful and great, is never going to get you wisdom. I can guarantee you that... Working is absolutely necessary. Otherwise, what do you expect? Enlightenment is not a gift, neither is liberation, or nirvana. You earn it. If it were a gift that Buddha could give you, he would have made gift parcels for everybody. But it doesn't work that way. It is your work to clear the obstacles and dirt out of your mind. When that is done you become pure. Your natural purity will connect with that and that is called enlightenment. I believe that is what enlightenment is all about. It is simple and straightforward, but working on it is difficult. "*[13]

Enlightenment is not a gift. Nirvana is not a gift. Becoming a vegan is not a gift. We have to put in some effort in if we want to change. We must work at it. It is hard to change a lifetime habit but compared to the goal of enlightenment it is easy and has great rewards from a health, ethical, environmental and altruistic standpoint.


## Analytical Antidote for Cheese

Cheese and dairy products in general seem to be the hardest foods to abandon eating. They are very addictive. They were the hardest foods for me to eliminate. The following is brief analytical meditation you can use which may help you to castoff all dairy products.

Imagine yourself at a great Italian restaurant whose pizza is exquisite, their sauce, their toppings and their dough is unrivaled. They serve only cow's cheese in the form of mozzarella. There are no vegan alternatives. You crave the cheese, you're ravenous for it, and you really want it. But you pause to consider it. What is it? Where did it come from? How did it get here in front of me? It does not come out of a refrigerated plastic bag; it comes from a cow's milk. It comes from a cow's milk which is destined for the cow's baby. Who was this cow? Does she suffer? Yes, she suffers. She suffers like every one of us who are sentient. She is sentient. But her suffering is more than the normal suffering of life and death, her suffering was added upon because her natural instincts and life have been stolen from her. The ability feed her baby has been stolen from her since her baby has been taken. She lamented, cried and looked for her baby for days. But her baby could not be found. Her baby could not be fed. Her baby could not be licked, cuddled and nurtured. Her milk is destined to become mozzarella cheese. It is not for her child. She is captive. She is not free. Her milk is stolen from her. If her baby is a male he will be dead soon and become veal. He will live a miserable life, chained by himself in a small enclosure. Alone and afraid he will look for his mother even as the slaughter's knife cuts his throat and he innocently will suck on his killer's fingers still searching his mother. If the baby is a female she will be taken and imprisoned for a few months and then become a captive for life as a milk cow, artificially impregnated against her will and have her offspring taken from her. The life of a dairy cow is a life of imprisonment. She will live in her own excrement and urine. She will suffer from mastitis, laminitis and other diseases from her life in a penitentiary called a "farm". Her life has been stolen from her. Her horns have been removed in a painful procedure. Her tail has been docked in a painful process that reverberates into suffering her entire life as she cannot swish flies that bite her during the summer months. She will be milked by machines which steal her children's milk and stores it in large refrigerated vats. Two or three times a day for her entire life she will be forced into the milking parlor to have her baby's milk drained from her body. This will occur until she can no longer stand from diseases of the hoof, or she cannot become impregnated and her milk dries up, or her milk slows as she gets older at the age of 3, 4 or 5. She will then be culled. She will also give up her life at the slaughterhouse at the hand of the butcher's knife to her throat. She will become low grade hamburger or dog food. This orphan who never knew her mother, who never knew her children and whose feminine body was misappropriated for my desire for mozzarella cheese on my pizza is a mother sentient being. She doesn't want to die; she gave her all in this life and in the end is slaughtered. I know that the first precept of the Buddha's teachings is to abstain from killing and I wonder if I am connected to this killing because I want mozzarella cheese? Yes, I am connected. The Buddha's second precept is to abstain from what is not freely given. Do I believe this poor sentient being gave up this milk destined for her kidnapped child freely? No, I know it was not given freely. The third precept tells us to abstain from sexual misconduct. Do I have connection to all the rapes this being has been forcibly made to endure over her short life and would I agree this would be OK if it was done to a human female? I am connected to her rapes and I never would support the rape of human beings. Looking into the crux of the fourth precept to train oneself to abstain from dishonesty, am I being honest with myself if I just eat the cheese? Am I choosing to mislead myself to believe there is such a thing as "humane" milk and "humane" cheese? Am I obscuring the truth and in a state of denial when I choose to ignore the confinement, cruelty and misery with which we inflict a life of hell and death on defenseless mother cows? Are a few pieces of mozzarella cheese pizza worth this suffering? No, I will skip the cheese because I do not want to be part of this structural violence any longer. I will remove myself from this group karma and learn to live without cheese and dairy products. I will sit here in my chair and focus on my resolution.

# The Ethical Mirror: The Five Precepts

As Carol J. Adams said,

*"If the problem is invisible, in a sense mirroring the physical invisibility of intensively farmed animals, then there will be ethical invisibility."*[14]

Pesky vegans, we make the problem visible. We bring visibility to unethical eating behavior; we question the status quo of eating meat, fish, dairy and eggs as necessary, normal, and OK. We make people uncomfortable with their choices just by our very presence. Veganism stands in indirect opposition with "Carnism", a term coined by Melanie Joy, Ph.D.[15] And that can be awkward when vegans and carnists come face-to-face in compassionate Buddhist Sangha's because when it comes to food choices, vegans are in direct alignment with the teachings on compassion, not killing, and awakening oneself, and non-vegans are not. Sometimes carnists are crabby. Sometimes they are rude. Sometimes they hide out. I understand they just don't want to be confronted with the fact that there is misery, death and cruelty on their plates. Ethical invisibility is comfortable.

Meriam-Webster defines ethics[16] in general as: rules of behavior based on ideas about what is morally good and bad; an area of study that deals with ideas about what is good and bad behavior; a branch of philosophy dealing with what is morally right or wrong; and a belief that something is very important. So what are Buddhist ethics and what type of behavior did the Buddha believe was good and bad?

Ethical behavior in Buddhism is based on compassion and wisdom as found in the Vinaya and the many precepts and vows taken by monks, nuns and lay people. There are numerous versions of these in the different branches of Buddhism but they all form the basis for decision making about one's own behavior. In Buddhist moralistic thought it is generally true that nothing is prescribed as an absolute good or an absolute bad, even killing another person when the slaying can save many other beings from death has some negativity involved. This is a very debatable subjective area. Buddhists are trained to decide their own moral behavior based on the precepts, logic, reason and compassion.

There are many various sets of vows and/or precepts in Buddhism: Pratimoksha vows, Bodhisattva vows, Tantric vows, lay person vows and between 218 to 380 different vows for monks and nuns. There are a myriad of lists: the three pure precepts (do no evil, do only good, save beings), the five precepts, the eight Mahayana precepts (in Tibetan Buddhism taken for 24-hours), the ten grave precepts, the 14, the 16, the 32, and then the 218, 263, 279 or 380 vows one takes if you are ordained.

One of the most basic and well known set of ethics in Buddhism for lay practitioners is comprehended in the five precepts: do not kill, do not steal, do not engage in sexual misconduct, do not lie, and do not use intoxicants. Each of these has layers upon layers of detail that are peeled away by the student over years of meditation practice. The five precepts help to guide our actions by helping us to understand whether an action will become harmful to us or the being(s) we are engaged with, i.e. will our action(s) cause suffering. These precepts can be viewed as the essential nucleus of the Buddha's teachings and his moral guidelines. They are not commandments as much as food for contemplation, for we know that as we live we do, undoubtedly, break the precepts. Following the teachings we become honest with ourselves and meditate on where we broke the precept and how we can change to not break the precept again. Used in this manner the precepts can form the basis for us to be more authentic with ourselves by becoming a person who does less and less harm. They allow us to face our feelings, lack of feelings, actions, lack of actions, and allow us to sit with ourselves to understand our negative emotions, states of mind and make changes. They allow us to examine and purify our actions by committing to not doing them again and in the process we become more mindful. They are designed to keep us mindfully present, moment by moment, so that we do not create unnecessary negativity in our lives. They are very different from the Ten Commandments, they are not engraved stone writings brought to us by a prophet upon a mountain but are terminologies of purpose, more like water than stone, as fluid guidelines of solidly grounded intentional purpose which are malleable and changeable based on situations and time. They must be dealt with from a seat of wisdom, intelligence and sensitivity as there can be situations where there is not a single course of action. Most importantly they must be used with utmost compassion for all other beings, the environment and ourselves.

# The First Precept

The first precept is: do not kill, refrain from killing, do not take part in killing, refrain from violence, embody non-violence, do not be an accessory to killing, do no harm, do not take life, do not destroy life and practice ahimsa. All of these statements symbolize the first precept and the express fact that all sentient beings suffer, want life, will cling to their lives with the last of their strength and in this we are all the same. This precept stands in direct opposition to eating meat, for as discussed sentient life includes ALL forms of life which have some semblance of consciousness, which means they have wants, needs, and can suffer. While there is some room for debate on this topic it is clear that insects, birds, squirrels, pigs, cows, elephants, wolves, dogs, cats, tigers, bears, deer, and fish are sentient. We can say with certainty the animals we consider food are sentient and when we choose to eat them we become accessories to their murder. We become killers of life when we participate in the collective murder through the market system as there would be no factory farms, slaughterhouses, and refrigerated packages of animal parts in stores if there were not eaters of meat. From the Dhammapada, 129-130, the Buddha is said to have taught that all beings tremble in front of danger and they all fear death and when we consider this, we who are mindful do not kill or cause others to kill. [17]

The positive counteraction to killing is love and compassion. When we realize we are all in the same boat we have love and compassion for others. But we cannot truthfully say to ourselves we have love and compassion when we eat animals because we cause their deaths.

Eating meat clearly makes us an accessory to their slaughter. As Roshi Phillip Kapleau states,

> *"To cause another to kill, torture, or harm any living creature likewise offends against the first precept. Thus to put the flesh of an animal into one's belly makes one an accessory after the fact of its slaughter, simple because if cows, pigs, sheep, fowl, and fish, to mention the most common, were not eaten they would not be killed."*[18]

# The Second Precept

The second precept is embodied by the following statements: do not steal, do not take what is not yours, do not take things not freely given, avoid stealing, train yourself not to steal, and avoid taking things without the permission of the owner. Stealing is wrong. I violated this precept every day of my life from a food standpoint until I became vegan. With every hamburger I ate, with every scoop of ice cream I consumed and with every omelet I downed, I desecrated this precept. And this takes us to a deeper meaning of this precept. It forces us to look deeper than the obvious. Sure we should not steal someone's car, jewelry, money and possessions but what about consideration for someone's stolen life? Did the dairy cow whose milk, cheese, butter, and ice cream I consumed give me permission to take her baby's milk? Did a mother cow give consent to have her baby taken? Did she give me permission to confine her in a factory farm against her natural instincts? Did she give consent to inject her with drugs, dehorn her, and force her to live on concrete? When she could no longer give milk and become impregnated, did she give consent for me to allow her to be slaughtered so that I could have cheap fast-food meat or use her body for dog food? Did she allow me to order her body at a fast-food restaurant in the form of a hamburger? Of course mother cows cannot give consent and never would if they could. We steal from them.

And what of the baby cow we have stolen her from her mother, who searches for her mother, and cries for her mother. Was the baby cow asked if we could take her away from her mother to become a dairy cow or veal? No, we steal from the baby cows too.

Stealing from animals breaks the second precept. Their children, milk, eggs, silk, wool, honey, lives, and happiness belong to them and we cause them great suffering when we steal. If they could answer the question can I have your eggs, your wool, your milk, and imprison you for your entire life they would certainly answer, no. They would not consent. They would remind us of the purposeful intention of the second precept and of nature's intention. A chicken or rooster would inform us "my egg is destined to become a sentient life form, a chicken and to live with other chickens free in the trees, caring for one another in flocks as we had for millennia." A mother cow would inform us, "my milk is intended for my baby cow that I carried for 9 months and gave birth to, not for humans." A queen bee would inform us, "our honey is intended to become food for our colony of bees, we worked diligently gathering pollen from thousands of flowers for months, and it is not intended for you to take. It is stealing."

Animals do not and would not give us their offspring, their secretions, and other substances they produce to care for themselves. It is pure larceny to take from them what is not given. It is absurd to think otherwise and on any level we cannot justify this theft. We who call ourselves Dharma practitioners, who do this unashamedly, violate and disrespect beings that cannot give their consent or defend themselves. The second precept does not say we can steal as long as we can rationalize or explain this violation and theft. It states: do not steal.

All the while we try to practice generosity, the opposite of stealing. As one of the six perfections (Six Paramitas) to which Buddhists aspire to, how can we believe we are being generous when we are accomplices to stolen babies, eggs, honey, fur, and lives? No hens would be made captive and no eggs would be stolen if we did not eat them. Eating another sentient being's eggs is not generous. Our habits make us accomplices to stealing from sentient life forms, the environment and our own health. As animals cannot give their consent we should never steal from them or we are guilty of breaking the Buddha's second precept and in direct opposition to perfecting generosity.

# The Third Precept

The third precept is: do not partake in acts of sexual misconduct, do not use sex as coercion, do not cheat sexually on someone when in a committed relationship, and do not have sex with someone who has not consented freely to the sexual activity. The essence of this precept is to not cause harm to ourselves and others. This precept not only relates to only human beings but animals too. The animals we use for food are repeatedly raped and forcibly impregnated. They are sentient and their sexual organs belong to them not us. This is true for cows, pigs, chickens, turkeys, and other farm animals. We use their reproductive organs, their sex organs, for producing offspring to generate money. We routinely commit sexual misconduct because they are not willing partners in the sexual acts we perform on them. What we do to these sentient beings is not congruent with the third precept. It should be clear to all that a mother cow put in the rape rack,[19] forcibly impregnated year-after-year (and whose baby is stolen from her) is a grievous transgression of the third precept. This action does not embody the spirit and intent of the third precept to keep our commitments in sexual relationships; it is the opposite as we become partners in violent rape against a sentient being who suffers considerably. Similarly when a mother pig is confined in a factory farm and repeatedly raped by artificial insemination to have dozens of piglets, this is done against her will, and is a misappropriation of her sexuality in order to increase the number of pigs in the population on the factory farm to be raised for slaughter (against the first precept). Her rape is performed for reasons of "production" in the industrial farming complex. How is the satisfaction of our appetite as dharma practitioners satiated when we know we are silent partners in sexual misconduct of others for our habit, taste, culture, and food preference? Does the rape of billions of sentient animals follow the purposeful intention of the third precept?

# The Fourth Precept

The fourth precept is: do not lie, do not be dishonest, avoid false speech, and do not hide the truth. This also means do not hide the truth of animal suffering from ourselves or others. Breaking the fourth precept was easy for me to do swathed in my cultural baggage with ruts deeper than a ten foot snow bank. I was blinded by habitual patterns and hid from myself through repressing and denying the damage I was doing to the environment, my health and animals by choosing to eat them. When I was in the habit of eating animals I repressed the truth, denied the truth and lied to myself.

Denial to oneself, actively or passively, is as much a part of the fourth precept as is denying the suffering of animals in modern factory facilities. We deny they are captive, deny they are suffering, deny we can do anything about their plight, and deny ourselves the ability to feel their suffering.

I have been known to post on Facebook gruesome photos and links to videos of factory farming and slaughter much to the dismay of other Buddhist practitioners who are my Facebook "friends". This has led to blocking, defriending, posting of negative commentary and fighting that end with comments similar to "I like bacon on my cheeseburger and even if I spend time in the hell realms, and I am going to go make one right now." Mostly the response is such that people explain they are weary of seeing reality. However, when we hide ourselves from the gruesome pictures and videos of cruelty on factory farms and yet continue to eat dairy products, meat, eggs and fish, we deny truth, we deny the ability to witness and sit with the suffering we cause. When we do this we deny our feelings. When we deny our feelings, we deny our full capacity to love. When we deny our feelings and full capacity to love, we deny ourselves the ability to awaken more completely. Truthfulness is the ethical counterpart to lying and is indispensable to an ethical life. How can we expect to be present, and aware, when we are not true to ourselves? How can we be in the "now" and use avoidance as a form of repressive denial?

Thich Nhat Hahn advises us, in the fourteen precepts of Interbeing, not to avoid any contact with suffering. We shouldn't close our eyes to suffering nor lose our awareness of its existence in the world. He goes further and tells us we should find ways to be with suffering, being with those whom suffer personally connecting with them through visits and not ignoring images, sound, and movies depicting suffering. These means are to be used to awaken ourselves to the reality of the First Noble Truth in the world today.[20]

## Humane Meat

And for those of us who accept the myth of "humane meat" and "cage free" eggs and other such industry media fabrications designated to soothe our consciousness we do ourselves an injustice. We continue to be part of the obscuration of truth partnering along with the industry whose primary focus is for us to continue to eat their product, their continued generation of profit, and not with full truthful disclosure.

We hide the truth from ourselves just as the industry conceals the unwilling captives behind the closed doors of factory farm buildings and slaughterhouses. There are no glass walls for factory farms as there are no glass walls in slaughterhouses. When we delude ourselves into believing the myth of humane slaughter (humane murder of a being against its will), humanely raised (confinement of a being against its will) we either have turned off our internal healthy dialogue or are speaking falsely ourselves -- and in direct opposition to the fourth precept. There is not any humanity in killing helpless vulnerable beings, there is not a single thing related to freedom, liberty and choice in confinement, and there is not any humanity in a slaughterhouse. There is no such thing as humane meat.

# The Fifth Precept

The fifth precept tells us: to not use intoxicants, mind-clouding substances, alcohol or drugs. It reminds us to respect one's mental health, one's awareness, and to not intoxicate ourselves with desire and heedlessness which can cause us to break the other 4 precepts. This means we should not use directly nor indirectly mind-clouding substances; as intoxicants can cause our judgment to fail and we lose our ability to evaluate what we are doing. In a word we become unmindful. This is the deeper meaning behind the $5^{th}$ precept. Alcohol or drugs that affect our mental stream may not be inherently bad but they can cloud our mind and we become addicted to their effects. When addiction kicks in we desire them more and more. Desire in and of itself clouds the mind and takes us out of the present moment. Desire is a key factor in any addiction as is pain. Once addicted we feed our holes with the object of our desire be it drugs, alcohol, money, or meat. Many of us fill our holes with food. Our addictions to the taste of meat, fish, eggs and dairy make us heedless to the first 4 precepts. The taste of a juicy rich cheeseburger sliding down our throats turns off consciousness and feeds our desire. We become unmindful of our participation of killing. We become unmindful of stealing. We become unmindful of lying. We become unmindful of the sexual misconduct of which we play a part. And if our addictions cloud the mind to this degree, is this not a flagrant example of intoxication?

Filling holes comes from pain. And pain comes from suffering. The wine of delusion is easy to drink when we turn our minds off and allow ourselves to become comfortably numb brainwashed in the sweet liquor of the media. We become drunk on war, terrorism, money, movies, sports, and products like the newest phone or tablet. Just as we become intoxicated with the love of bacon, cheeseburgers, lamb chops and lobster.

However, the positive counterpart to the fifth precept is awareness and mindfulness. But under the influence of desire we are not aware of our suffering and the suffering of others. We are not mindful.

So what does someone who purports to follow the direction of the Buddha do? What would Buddha do? Be mindful. Sit, meditate, follow the precepts through mindfulness and change our moral status. Just so the Mahayana precepts state,

> *"From now on I shall not kill, nor steal others' possessions, nor engage in sexual conduct, nor lie. I shall avoid intoxicants from which many mistakes arise... As Arhats have avoided wrong actions such as taking the lives of others, I shall also avoid such actions as taking the lives of others. May I quickly obtain enlightenment and may the living beings who are experiencing the various sufferings be released from the ocean of samsara."*[21]

Implementing the five precepts means analyzing each and every moment in our lives. We need to be aware and encounter each action we take as an opportunity to learn and change. Moment-by-moment we have the ability to be fearless, honest and embody truth. If we see our actions, behavior and mind is causing suffering we should stop and understand the ethical morality of the situation.

Morality, it is said, is the foundation for all virtue. It is the centerpiece for all enlightened activity. As Narjuna[22] states in a letter to friend:

> *"You should practice a morality unbroken, not debased.*
> *Undefiled, untainted, uncorrupted,*
> *Morality was declared the foundation of all virtue,*
> *Just as the earth is for all things moving and unmoving."*[23]

Basic morality unbroken is outlined by the five precepts and when followed, we learn to avoid non-virtues, accumulate good works/merit and watch our mind closely.

The five precepts are not about moderation. Moderation is a convenient excuse I have used. The middle path is not about acceptance of suffering. Killing, stealing, lying, sexual misconduct and heedlessness have no moderate middle path of acceptance or we run the risk of being blind to our own delusions, desires, attachments and aversions.

When we claim to love animals, but we continue to consume cheese, milk, ice cream or any dairy product are we being truthful? How can this be truthful when we are active accomplices in victimizing mother cows? How can we be in love and at peace with anyone we are victimizing?

Have you ever boiled a living being alive? When I was a child around age 10, my friends and I, captured bees, put them in a glass jar with holes on top. We threw them into a fire and watched them die. This only happened once as I felt instant terrible regret and remorse. I never did it again and today I grow flowers to help bees and other pollinators. But little did I know, I still continued to be an accomplice to boiling animals alive. Every time I ate chicken, pork or lobster or other animals I was a co-conspirator. Every day across the country, fully-conscious pigs and chickens are submerged into blistering, hot water. As pointed out in Slaughterhouse by Gail A. Eisnitz,

> *"Other industrialized nations require that chickens be rendered unconscious or killed prior to bleeding and scalding, so they won't have to go through those processes conscious. Here in the United States, however, poultry plants— exempt from the Humane Slaughter Act and still clinging to the industry myth that a dead animal won't bleed properly—keep the stunning current down to about one-tenth that needed to render a chicken unconscious."*[24]

Additionally Gail A. Eisnitz uncovered worker testimony[25] revealing that fully conscious pigs are routinely dunked, in hair removal scalding tanks which are 140 degrees Fahrenheit. This is a common practice to dunk pigs that have been stunned and bled, but stunners cannot keep up with the rapid pace of a new hog to stun every four seconds, especially with electrical charges set too low. Hogs are stunned electrically rather than mechanically (with bolt guns) at John Morrell and Company and the company regularly lowers the voltage on stunners to eliminate the possibility of "Bloodspash" a condition which can occur when a pig is excessively prodded down the chute to its death or if the stunner improperly applied the electrodes to the animal. "Bloodspash" or "blown loins" make the meat look discolored and blood-stained and thus not able to be sold at the highest rates. Imagine you are in the shower and someone turns the water to scalding hot. We all freak out when the water is too hot, but we can move and change the temperature, pigs cannot. Imagine you are hung by one of your legs from a moving chain fully conscious and unable to escape? This is just part of the plight of pigs.

How can we love someone and boil him or her alive? Or cause another human to boil him or her alive for us? If you eat chicken or pigs you support the boiling of sentient beings alive.

Living is action. Action can be positive or negative, hurtful or helpful, and it can cause more harm or less harm. Our action can have either harmful or beneficial consequences. The role of intention plays a big part in the gravity of our actions, and their karmic effect. Conscious intention can be positive or negative. Wanting to kill and then killing is premeditated murder and is the most negative action in Buddhism. Not wanting to kill and unintentionally killing is a less serious offense. Just as in court rooms, so it is with karma. Denial is a form of repressed intention; we know the truth but do not want to face it. But just because it causes too much cognitive dissonance or pain does not mean it takes the action out of the realm of premeditation. We know when we go to a restaurant and order a double-cheeseburger that an animal has suffered, another animal will suffer, and perhaps the provider of the cheese is still suffering. We become part of the issue by being a consumer and just because we choose to deny, suppress, and ignore the truth of the moment when we order and eat this food does not take away the terrible negativity. We act as though we are not killing with intent, but we are the ones ordering the food and entering the marketplace for sentient beings to be caged, imprisoned, tortured and murdered. It is done on our behalf. When we bite into the sandwich we get great satisfaction and should not kid, fool and make ourselves unwise by acting as though we are not part of the problem. I was. We are. This is a form of conscious intention. To eat meat in 2015 and consider it unintentional is to discredit, dishonor and rebuke the teaching of the Buddha and the five precepts. Sitting in a restaurant eating the corpse of a suffering being and the melted secretions of misery are not the practice of Ahimsa. You have become the opposite of holy person, as the Buddha stated:

> "He who has renounced violence toward all beings weak or strong who neither kills nor causes to kill, him do I call a holy man."[26]

The five precepts are a description of how an enlightened being lives. For the rest of us they describe a path of self-discipline, training, and hard work to embody. The precepts are part of the path to achieve enlightenment. They cause us to become more mindful, generous, truthful, content, and less violent. We will fail and fall off the bike often as we try to ride down the path. We must pick ourselves up when we fall and not beat ourselves up but start pedaling again.

Buddhists, Buddhist-vegans and vegans do not and cannot follow the precepts perfectly. I personally fail in many ways. Thich Nhat Hahn has stated that he cannot follow these precepts perfectly. He admits he fails in many ways each and every day but suggests these are goals for which we should strive to fulfill. They are our practice and only practice can make these words become true. [27]

As the moral path of the precepts opens in front of us we learn that when we kill, we are killing ourselves. We learn that when we steal we are stealing from ourselves. We learn that if we desire another person's possessions and misappropriate their bodies in a clear act of sexual misconduct we become less contented and harm ourselves. We learn that if we lie we continue to delude ourselves and stay ignorant by our own choosing. And if we become drunk on the theories, models, and pronouncements heaped upon us by modern media whose droning is, in countless cases, the lip service of the agribusiness, chemical, pharmaceutical, medical, corporate, military, governmental multiplex we learn we've lost our ability to see clearly for ourselves. Being responsible for our actions is the way a Buddhist practitioner purifies and makes changes to him or herself. Karma will occur and we must decide if we want it to continue. We must decide if eating animals is a responsible thing to do. We must analyze whether eating meat, fish, dairy, and eggs arises out of a condition of suffering or out of the seat of compassion. We must decide if we want to create more harm in the world or less harm in the world. In terms of what we choose to eat in 2015, where one has the means to choose, there is only one course of action that embodies the five precepts and that is a vegan way of eating and living.

# Why Aren't Buddhists Leading the Vegan Movement?

*"Buddhism ought to be an animal rights religion par excellence. It teaches the unity of all life, it holds kindness and compassion to be the highest virtues; and it explicably includes animals in its moral universe. Buddhist rules of conduct – including the First Precept, 'Do not kill' – apply to our treatment of animals as well as our treatment of human beings. This would lead us naturally to expect Buddhists to oppose all forms of animal exploitation."* Norm Phelps, <u>The Great Compassion</u>[28]

Buddhism is in direct opposition to exploitation of sentient beings. Veganism is in direct opposition to exploitation of sentient beings. It would seem that veganism and Buddhism support each other and would be wholly embraced by the Buddhist community of teachers, monks, nuns and lay followers. But sadly it is not and many of the basic reasons are desire, willful addiction, aversion, attachment and ignorance. In other words many like the taste, have a habit and see animals as "others". One hears all the time things such as, "I love the taste of bacon", "I've always eaten this way", and "the being is already dead and I didn't kill it." This uncanny blind spot plays out for some of the following reasons:

# Health

We believe meat is needed for health even when it has been proven, time and time again, fruits, vegetables, grains, and legumes provide superior health benefits and whereas animals products are associated with disease. For every scientific study claiming the benefits of animal products, there are dozens showing plants provide greater benefits. Plants have every nutrient needed for a healthy body including protein, fiber, vitamins and minerals with the sole exception of vitamin $B_{12,}$ which must be supplemented. To continue to believe animals products (the bodies of sentient beings) are needed for optimum health is to, put frankly, is an ignorant belief. Plants provide powerful protection from a variety of disease states including certain cancers, heart disease, diabetes, obesity, autoimmune diseases, bone, kidney, eye and brain diseases.[29] The health aspects of eating meat versus the eating of a whole-foods-plant-based-diet are explored in great detail in The Buddha, The Vegan and You, Part II. The bottom-line is that a whole-foods plant-based diet is associated with health whereas a diet containing animal products is associated with disease promotion. Meat, fish, dairy and eggs are not health food.

# Protein Deficiency

We believe we will not get enough protein if we don't eat animals. But strangely enough no one I have ever met knows of a person who has died from a protein deficiency. Personally I have not eaten an animal product in over five years and I have no protein deficiency. On the contrary, my health has improved. I know vegans who have not eaten an animal product in 30 to 40 years with no negative protein deficiency effects. The reality is protein is in every single plant-based whole-food, especially leafy greens which have more protein per calorie than beef.[30]

# Culture

Most of us come from meat eating cultures which have three features in common: 1) a learned habit and taste, 2) societal status and, 3) health myths.

When you are brought up in a meat eating culture it is hard to change your eating habits. We learn from our culture it is "OK" to eat meat and at a young age we form habits which stay with us for lifetimes. It's really that simple. When we come from meat eating cultures it is challenging to become vegan because we miss home and want to go home every day with our meals. Home is comfort. If home was a meat-eating place then meat is comfort food. We all tend toward that which makes us feel comfortable, even violent practices and environments.

There is also the stigma of wealth and prestige which comes with eating meat in many cultures. I remember my grandmother who came from a dirt poor family in Calabria, Italy, stating she always knew it was a holiday because there was the luxury of a piece of meat on the dinner table. Being from a high-status family and not eating meat takes a person down a rung in society, they are not the same "privileged" individual anymore. Coming from lower status families and being able to eat meat means you are moving up in society. In some ways the ability to have meat on your table is a symbol of status. Meat is thus status. People are attracted to status.

As discussed, it is believed meat is healthy, that we need meat to get protein, and that to have strong blood we need to eat meat. Even the physicians of His Holiness the Dalai Lama believe he must eat meat to be healthy and fight his hepatitis virus.[31] All these myths have been debunked by modern science yet they still exist.

## Counterfeit Harmony -- Lead by Example and Keep Quiet

I was recently told in private, after a dinner out with a dozen or so sangha members, that I should, *"Lead by my example and not discuss veganism. It's not harmonious."* This was spoken by a practitioner who I believe felt uncomfortable with the food on her plate and conversations about compassionate eating. Even though this discussion was initiated by someone else in the group and never directed toward her, she needed to tell me I was not creating harmony.

In order to preserve harmony within a group some feel it is better to not speak up after all the Buddha did not create disharmony. In general, while it is difficult to understand each situation and to know when it is wise to speak and when it is prudent to be silent, there are some who believe we should only lead by quiet example when it comes to not eating animals. However, I am not sure the Buddha and Buddhist teachings inform us to be quietly harmonious in the face of enslavement, exploitation, and killing of any sentient beings -- people or animals. The preservation of harmony through complicit silence toward suffering begets false approval. It may be easier to stay silent but as Martin Luther King said, "Our lives begin to end the day we become silent about things that matter."[32] Likewise, 2,600 years earlier, the Buddha informs us in the Brahmajala Sutra, to "devise skillful" methods to protect animals: *"Whenever Bodhisattvas see a person preparing to kill animals, they should devise a skillful method to rescue and protect them, freeing them from their suffering and difficulties."*[33] In our 2015 database driven corporate society of consumption this means we are duty-bound to not sidestep the emotional discomfort of the confrontation of others be they students, monks and/or instructors as eating meat, fish, dairy and eggs means more animals will become victimized. Therefore, silence in these instances renders us complicit with captivity, mistreatment, and suffering.

When I don't speak out for those who cannot, the animals on our plates, I know I feel inside me a sense of counterfeit harmony. *"Counterfeit harmony"* is a term coined by a spiritual friend, Tashi Nyima whereby he posits it is our job to speak up and not be silent in the face of brutality. As Tashi Nyima has so aptly put it,

> *"In order to preserve a counterfeit harmony, some persons hold that the Buddha instructed us to be silent in the face of blatant misrepresentations of the Dharma, such as the deceptive reasoning of those who pretend that the cruel enslavement, exploitation, and slaughter of animals is approved by the Buddha. Such persons place the temporary emotional discomfort of their Dharma teachers and Sangha peers over the unspeakable suffering of non-*

*human animals. This complicit timidity is contrary to the Dharma. Each person must come to his/her own conclusions, but we must never be silent in the face of violence. Respectfully, but boldly, we must speak up for ALL sentient beings:*

*'Such speech as the Tathagata knows to be true, correct, and beneficial, even if unwelcome and disagreeable to others, the Tathagata knows the time to use such speech. Why is that? Because the Tathagata has compassion for all beings.* - Buddha Shakyamuni, Middle Length Discourses'"

Humbleness and gentleness should not be confused with silence when being confronted by bloodshed. Silence is the response of someone full of fear, not the way of Buddha or an engaged practitioner. And while we should not meet brutality with violence we should also not meet it with complicit silence. Rather we should meet it with unflinchingly respectful language which is clear and concise. If we believe that the eating of sentient beings is a *"blatant misrepresentation of the Dharma,"* then it's our responsibility to speak up and not preserve *"counterfeit harmony"*.

## Empty-Heart

There are some Buddhists who point toward the doctrine of emptiness as a reason for eating meat as "it makes no difference since all things are empty." This analysis is flawed and excludes suffering as part of reality. In ultimate reality, emptiness, they reason everything is "bliss and nirvana" so these Buddhists feel like they can eat what they want since it really doesn't matter. *"Everything is empty, don't you know."*

This is a complete misunderstanding of emptiness because suffering is real and ignoring suffering is disregarding the First Noble Truth. Additionally, suffering, which is experienced in relative reality, is part and parcel of sphere of emptiness which is an expansive point of view beyond words and cognition which must be experienced to comprehend. While there may not be suffering when one is in a state of direct experience of emptiness, emptiness does not negate the suffering of those who cannot encounter this state of being. Perhaps Buddhists who believe this should check their hearts and brains as they may be empty of true understanding and devoid of altruistic aspiration. To ignore suffering and base one's right to eat meat on emptiness seems to denote a glaring absence of compassion. As Guru Rinpoche Padmasambhava, has stated, *"Although your view may be higher than the sky, your conduct must be finer than flour."*

## Not Necessary

We believe it's not necessary to change; we can simply keep doing what we are doing and reach an awakened state. We are unwilling to change. We believe since we are not doing the killing ourselves we are somehow exonerated from any connection to the beings we eat. This certainly flies in the face of dependent origination[34].

# Fear

We are afraid to change and think we will get sick. Some of us do get sick and actually feel like we go through withdrawal when not eating animals and their secretions. I had a conversation with a long time practitioner at St. Peters (not Rome, but Corktown in Detroit) and I remember the student relaying their experience while attending a 3-week retreat at Plum Village in France. At Plum Village, a vegan Buddhist center, the student didn't have any access to meat, fish, eggs or dairy. After 3-days headaches, chills and nausea set in. They were quite sick from lack of animal products. So sick they needed to travel to the nearest village to purchase cheese. When I postulated the possibility of detox I was met with some incredulity as was the suggestion of breaking an addictive habit.

# My Teacher Eats Meat

Some practitioners use the excuse that "my teacher eats meat" or "my teacher told me I need to eat meat when I am not feeling well", which ends all conversation when the lama or guru herself or himself eats meat. Of course teachers don't want to be alone in their meat eating habits and if they do eat meat, well so can you!

However profound respect for your teacher can still exist just because you do not choose to eat meat and follow their example. It does not break the bond between student and teacher. It's OK not to follow everything the teacher does. We have our own minds and our own path. If a teacher tells you to eat meat you can kindly and politely say "No, I would like to listen to you but I respectfully must decline." Your pure relationship should still be intact if the teacher has the qualities necessary to be a spiritual guide. Honesty and a straightforward communication are best and produce a wholesome relationship. So if the teacher eats meat you don't have to follow his or her example in this area and a deep respect toward this person can still exist.

## Monks Eat Meat

This is related to "my teacher eats meat" and is used to justify one's own habits because if monks who took 200 or more vows can do this, then so can I.

## Reincarnation is a Myth

Some feel like the whole reincarnation idea and that all beings have been our mother is a myth. They don't come from Indian, Chinese or Japanese culture and deep down they just are not buying it. "All beings have been my mother and have been kind to me," is a nice story but bringing this teaching into one's own core set of beliefs and values is another thing indeed, especially when it means I cannot eat them.

## Don't Care

Some don't want to change and even state unequivocally they gladly will suffer the consequences, if there are any in hell realms or other karmic penalties. In other words, they like meat and don't care to stop and are determined to continue. Many times these conversations end in, "Now I am going to have a cheeseburger with extra bacon on top."

# What Can I Do?

Many believe their small effect, that just they themselves changing will not make much of a difference. They state, "The world is such a mess, what can I do?" as in, we personally can only impact slightly the global issue of meat eating. What can I do is related to the next category, "I only eat a little bit". However, if analyzed from the animal's point of view we see things completely different.

# I Only Eat A Little Bit

Many fellow Dharma practitioners only eat a little bit of meat, little dairy and very small amounts of fish. Somehow a little bit eases their consciousness. Certainly a little bit is better than a lot, but here is the issue: a little bit still kills the entire animal, stills abuses the sentient being, still causes suffering to the sentient life form. When well meaning "little bit" eaters multiply themselves by millions, then billions of sentient beings become a calamitous blood-spattered result.

# The Three Rules

Others recite the three rules the Buddha is said to have laid out, if it wasn't killed for you, and you didn't see or hear the animal being slaughtered, it is OK to eat the meat. This is also very convenient today with slaughterhouses, meat packing houses being so far away. Not to mention refrigeration is everywhere. However when analyzed against modern culture, the three rules are irrelevant and a flagrant excuse to continue to have sentient beings on one's plate.

## The Buddha Ate Meat

The reason some proclaim the Buddha ate meat is very similar to my teacher eats meat and ends all conversation, or attempts to. Also it is often stated the Buddha ate pork the day before he died and it was poisonous food. If he ate meat, I can too, and therefore reason, logic and compassion can be set aside. The fact that this story may well be just that a fictional story, told by meat-eating Buddhist scribes to justify their own desires and habit, is not discussed. The need to use one's own brain in the present day world is also set aside. The fact of the matter is that times have changed and it is irrelevant today if the Buddha ate meat, condoned it or not.

## Science Says "Animals Don't Suffer"

Many do not believe that animals actually suffer much and link themselves to old scientific theories that have been debunked. René Descartes thought animals were machines who did not feel pain, their struggles being simply automatic responses without feelings. These Buddhist-Cartesian minds are stuck in sixteenth century and mechanistic theories. They don't want to face the suffering of animals and hide out with this old thought pattern taught in the West.

# Scholars Confirm Early Buddhists Ate Meat

And just to confirm that meat eating is not a negative thing and common to Buddhists all over the world scholars confirm the misconception that Buddhists are vegetarian.[35] Many scholars reference the historical role of monks and nuns as wandering mendicants from Sramana,[36] ascetic traditions that had renounced all worldly attachments and had no job, no belongings but a robe and bowl and subsisted on alms. Alms were a form of generosity and provided great merit for the giver. If villagers were restricted in what they could offer, this would restrict the amount of merit they could receive. This is one historical reason given as to why the Buddha did not require his followers to be vegetarians. Times were tough 2,500 years ago. Thus Devadatta, the Buddha's vilified cousin, who practiced the five austerities was refused the request he made to the Buddha to require all followers to be vegetarian. It turns out that one of the "five severe types of austerities" included vegetarianism. The ease and variety of available vegetarian food makes this reasoning laughable, however I feel the alms reasoning still applies and thus if you subsist by alms alone as a wandering mendicant today, accept what is given. If you do not subsist on alms in 2015 this historical reasoning is no more than an excuse without compassion. Veganism is not a severe austerity today; it is easy, healthy and environmentally sound.

The bottom-line is that many students of the Buddha do not seem to believe the teachings of the Buddha, the Mahayana path, and are not genuinely honest with themselves. Due to ignorance they do not implement the teachings on compassion. They do not utilize reason and logic. They are simply going through the motions and selectively ignoring portions of the teachings as they relate to their tastes and habit (desire and addiction). They are stuck in their ways and use convenient excuses to continue eat meat, fish, dairy and eggs, thereby causing suffering to others.

There are a few voices with a positive message on this subject in the world of Buddhism today. Many teachers affirmatively acknowledge, if asked, that a vegan diet is the most compassionate way to eat -- they themselves do not eat a vegan diet. And so all-in-all Buddhists are not leading the vegan movement, even though compassion is core to all spiritual development and even though ethical living forms the basis for learning and building upon one's personal foundation of compassion.

And while Buddhists are not leading the vegan movement, may not want to know the full truth, and prefer to stay ignorant, comfortable, and numb, this is about to radically change. The voices making a connection to the food we eat and the beings who must suffer are getting louder. After all, animals on our plates are not food, they are violence.

Special Note: The Dharma Voices for Animals organization and the teachers affiliated with it are one compassionate haven and refuge. They are a Dharma organization whose global mission is to bring awareness to these important issues. They are not a vegan or vegetarian organization although they espouse both diets as leading to a more compassionate way of eating and living. They have produced a wonderful fifty minute video entitled, The Buddha and Animals. You can view the video and learn

more        about        their        mission        at:
*www.dharmavoicesforanimals.org*

# Why are there Sentient Beings on my Plate and Why I am "OK" With It?

We are taught as Buddhist practitioners to meditate on loving kindness for all beings and we start with those in our inner circle who have been the kindest. The most basic form of this is to think of our mother (or our most precious caregiver) and her love for us. She carried us for nine months through the three trimesters with their requisite aches, pains, and discomfort. When we were inside her she ate the best foods to keep us healthy. Always, and with every decision, she had us on her mind, her precious child. She struggled and suffered with our birth for hours. If the birth was caesarean she was cut open so that we could come out into the world. She nurtured us with the warmth of her body, the milk from her breasts, and the love in her heart. She cleaned us, taught us, supported us in every way until we were able to go to school and continued this until we were able to take care of ourselves. She taught us how to walk, how to eat and what to eat. If not for her kindness we would not know how to speak, read, clean ourselves, and love. All these things we did not come into this world knowing. It is the love of our mother who provided for all this, through years of hardships and difficulty. She always saw us as her most precious, always wanted to take care of us, and guard us day and night.

When we meditate on a mother's love we realize we would not be alive if it was not for her kindness or the kindness of those who are like a mother in our lives. The teachings of the Buddha inform us that throughout endless time we have had many mothers and that all beings have at one point or another been our mothers and taken care of us in this same manner. All mothers have shown us nothing but love and put us first and foremost above their own needs. When we meditate on this the question arises how can we be unkind, mistreat, or cause hurt for anyone or any being? As all beings have taken care of us, given us everything we need to live and be happy. We should acknowledge this includes all the beings unfortunate enough to be born as a "food animal" in the factory farm slaughterhouse industrial complex of our modern world.

The teachings inform us it is only through lack of awareness, to the love we have been shown, that we can be unkind. In my own personal instance, it was only through lack of awareness that I repaid their kindness by ordering them up at a restaurant to become the food I ate. It was through lack of awareness I bought their body parts in little Styrofoam packages covered with plastic at the grocery store, brought them home, and cooked them. It was through lack of awareness I was able to purchase their milk in plastic jugs to drink. It was through lack of awareness that when I ate animal products I ignored the fact another animal was being ordered up, born, and grown to become a fattened baby and slaughtered for my benefit in the meat-medical-pharmaceutical complex we live in today. It was only through lack of awareness that I believed I could become Buddha-like, a kinder more gentle person, a person who helps more and creates less harm in the world, growing in merit and becoming a benefit to myself and others, while still eating mother sentient beings. It was only through lack of awareness that I believed I could love beings and eat them.

When I look back as a supposed Bodhisattva in training, a person who wished to become awake, fully loving and having compassion for all beings, I wonder how I thought I could become awake in my day-to-day activities and relationships when I had animals on my plate. I wondered how I could "be there" for others when I was not awake enough to be there for the beings at the end of my fork. I wonder how if I disregarded mother sentient beings by eating them, where my disregard stopped. I remember how easily I remained comfortably numb as a part of the meat-medical-pharmaceutical complex all the while wishing for progress along the path. It was only when I stopped wishing and started acting with compassion in this area by taking the vegan challenge that I awoke from this horror. I was not being genuine. I was not implementing the teachings of the Buddha by eating sentient beings. I was doing the opposite. I was the cause of more, unnecessary, suffering in the world.

# Mindful Eating: Being Genuine, Honest and Forthright

The teachings of the Buddha point us toward becoming more genuine, honest, and forthright with ourselves. This is the route of morality as guided by the precepts with the teachings leading us to become more thoughtful, feeling, and alert as we meditate. They teach us to look deeply, breathe deeply and make space for our own inner exploration. They teach us that we don't have to do anything except to be here and now fully resting in the present moment. When we do so we become fully genuine, honest and forthright finding that the truth of any matter eventually presents itself, the compassionate next steps and the skillful next steps present themselves. In this state of mind we are able to act with more compassion and less drama. Being genuine, honest and forthright means we are more able to see our issues from other angles and vantages formerly unseen. It gives us some rope to unwind ourselves and just be whom we are, truly compassionate, wholesome, and wise humane beings who wish to help, and have the capacity to help others and our own selves. When we become more genuine, honest and forthright we see the truth of a matter, be it what is on your plate, what is happening in a relationship, or anything else in life. Being genuine, honest and forthright is possible without doing anything except breathing, sitting, and watching your mind. It is meditation without the formal sitting.

When we are genuine about what we eat, we see what is on our plates for what it is. When we are fully honest: we know where it came from and how it got there. If there are animal products on our plates we know someone suffered, was tortured, was probably raped, and certainly had to die. When there are no animal products on our plates we know there was no one who had to directly suffer, be imprisoned, raped and die.

When we are genuine and honest with ourselves and see that there is suffering on our plates, we seek to comprehend the causes and conditions of such suffering. Even if when we find out, we are uncomfortable. When we begin to become uncomfortable then we are onto something and have something further to meditate on. Whenever I have found something that is uncomfortable it leads me to something I want to deny and leave hidden.

There is a negative emotion lurking in the shadows which I should be confronting with a genuine, honest, open, forthright attitude. Ignorance can be that simple, we are uncomfortable, and we want to "ignore-ance" the entire situation. I know, that just in this way, I wanted to repress the knowledge of what was on my plate.

So when you look at your plate and see suffering where does it lead you? Do you want to deny the suffering, move on, do what is comfortable and eat the food? Do you want to explore it further and find out perhaps how much suffering occurred, to find out the causes and conditions of the food you eat?

Being genuine and honest means you do care, you do want the truth, you do seek the truth and you are a willing witness. It means being fully present not fearful to stand up or to change based on what you have found. It is a state where you are able to relate without fear, retaliation, or hatred as you are fully present with the First Noble Truth.

# Practicing Conflicted and Contradicted

I know well, as we should if we watch our thoughts, the mind state of "not present", which is also not genuine and stuck in a repressed rut. I was a conflicted and contradicted practitioner, when it came to eating meat, fish, dairy and eggs. As most of the teachings, practices, and meditation prayers inform us not to cause harm, I ate meat, fish, dairy and eggs in direct contradiction to the teachings. On a daily basis starting at 5:00 am I would sit on a cushion meditating and reciting phrases like:

"In my heart I turn to the Three Jewels of refuge.
May I free suffering beings and place them in
bliss.
May the compassionate spirit of love grow within
me.
That I may complete the enlightening path."

And:

"By means of holding both sutra and tantra,
May I liberate all living beings completely"

And:

"To the Three Gems I go for refuge,
All beings I shall liberate
And place in the state of awakedness,
The Bodhichitta I shall fully generate."

And:

"By the virtue of this practice, may I... liberate all
sentient beings."

I recited, meditated upon, sat with and prayed for all to be liberated for years but I never fully made the connection between eating beings at lunch and what I was stating over and over again in my morning's intentions. I was learning to sit and meditate, but was my compassion expanding? I thought just sitting every day, feeling good about being a nice person, going about my commitment to meditate that I was actually doing some good in the world. I was after all keeping my commitments every day, helping my family, giving to charities, not killing by putting bugs outside, feeding the birds, loving my dogs, and avoiding squirrels in the road. I was enthusiastic about the practices, trying hard to curb my anger, trying hard to realize my faults by pointing the finger back at myself, trying to identify my own blind spots, neuroses and ego grasping ways. Wasn't this the pathway to liberating all sentient beings including myself? It didn't dawn on me either that I was stopping my own progress and that there was an easy to fix to bring myself into greater moral alignment. It didn't dawn on me I just needed to stop eating animals—until I actually stopped eating them.

Looking back I remember feeling I was making some progress but my moral compass was not in alignment with my outer "eating" activity. Was this a prelude to becoming an ethical vegan?

## Samsaric Delusion

My father, who was diagnosed with schizophrenia in his early 20s, committed suicide when I was 4-years-old. He suffered for many years with this malady until he could not take the suffering any further. Schizophrenia is a mental disorder frequently characterized by abnormal social behavior and failure to recognize what is real. Schizophrenics are delusional. He and his twin brother (who did not commit suicide) had common symptoms of false beliefs, unclear and confused thinking, auditory hallucinations, issues with social engagement and emotional expression, and periods of completely shutting down. Sometimes I feel that our entire society is turned upside down on the issue of eating animals and are unable to see what is real. We hold dearly onto the false belief that incarcerating and murdering billions of animals, and then eating their bodies is somehow normal. We are confused in our thinking and shut down in our emotional expression when it comes to food. We say one thing and do another and we believe our delusions.

In food choice, I certainly was a delusional Buddhist practitioner, as is any who eats animals but has the wherewithal to choose otherwise. I loved animals, prayed for animals, and ate animals. I had an inner me and an outer me. I had a far-reaching failure in my ability to recognize what was real. I was not whole, but fragmented. I did not cause less harm, I caused more harm. I was under the mass-delusion we experience around the eating of meat and the garden variety breakage of the fifth precept—intoxication with my delusion. I spoke one way and acted another. When one compares vegan Buddhists to non-vegan Buddhists we find they have the same definition of compassion. They are not dissimilar. But meat eating Buddhists are deluded in many cases and when we start listing off who is on the receiving end of compassion we may perhaps notice something remarkable. The following dialogue between two practitioners brings out this point:

> "Maybe my understanding of kindness and compassion differs from yours', said the non-vegan to a vegan.
> The two started comparing who is on the receiving end of their compassion: children, parents, relatives, friends, community, human beings in general, animals and all sentient life.
> The non-vegan mentioned all kinds of animals, dogs, cats, wolves, bears, etc. and then said 'Actually, I love all animals'.

The vegan then asked, 'How about the animals you eat and use, the chicken on your plate and the leather coat on your back?'

There was a deadening silence.

The vegan said, 'See, your understanding of kindness and compassion does not differ from mine. It differs from your own'."

This dialogue brings out a blind spot in Buddhism today. Depending on what sangha you belong to and whom your teacher is, there can be almost a complete disregard for what is on our plates. We contemplate and try to cultivate patience, generosity, enthusiasm, meditation, discipline and the other perfections but we don't want to look at what is right in front of us. And there are too few teachers ready point this issue out, perhaps it so hard to collect students and followers (and membership fees) we just don't want to turn donors off?

# Blind Buddhas – The Buddhist Blind Spot, The Focus on Human Beings

The teachings I have studied and been blessed to receive since 1997 are truly a compassionate framework for living one's life. One troublesome area is however the primary emphasis on human beings. Teachers, books, podcasts, videos, and retreats from many traditions have this in common. This emphasis causes a blind spot for the practitioners when it comes to animals and supports a feeling of superiority to other life. It seems to play to our need for ego gratification and into the western sensibilities of food, food in the form of cows, pigs, chickens, fish, dairy and eggs as something for "us" humans to eat. It's a nice neat package. On the one hand we have enlightened compassionate masters and meditation teachers who are telling us it's our job to be compassionate, lose our ego and change ourselves and on the other we have them telling us (silently or vocally) it's OK to eat meat which is what we want to hear. So why change this habit we love when they inform us we can be compassionate and still eat sentient beings?

According to the Buddhist cosmology and belief in reincarnation there are various realms that consciousness can become born into: hell realms, ghost realms, the animal realm, the human realm and god-like realms. It's said that the human realm is the best realm because there is enough suffering that we look for a way out, we have the capacity to awaken, are motivated to seeking freedom, question our whole existence, and are eager existential beings searching for answers. We also, if luckily enough to have time, are endowed with the mental and emotional capabilities to break through and become an awakened Buddha. On the other hand, it is taught, if you're in a hell realm you don't have time because of the endless suffering, or if you're in an animal realm you don't have the mental capacity to think, reason and meditate, and if in a god-like realm you're so happy and content you don't have any motivation to inquire and seek change. You're simply not interested. Humans are thus elevated to a status of "those who can become Buddha" and this makes us special. This creates an opportunity for a blind pedestal to develop. If taken too far it can lead to speciesism.

This pedestal that human beings are put upon leads to a comfortable rut, it doesn't challenge us to think outside the box, such as, the outrageous thought that other beings are not here to be our food. Indeed when numerous practitioners hear stories about someone thinking outside of the box like this, they question it. Not wanting to eat animals, being a vegan, becomes something to defend as a vegan practitioner. It's pretty funny and poignant when one's compassion must be defended. It becomes something turned against vegans as they are now judged to be "attached to veganism". Because of *"your attachment"* it becomes something negative. Vegans attached to plant foods become negativity while the norm of eating animals, animals that must die to become food, is viewed as non-attachment and a personal choice. This situation is so comfortable even vegan friendly practitioners sometimes cannot see past their own bias. This causes the few vegans in these spiritual communities to have to defend their positions of not killing. And this is a global commonplace phenomenon, as I have heard this from practitioners not only in the U. S. and North America, but Europe, Asia, South America, and Australia.

The following conversation occurred at a recent retreat where three practitioners were standing around the proverbial "water cooler" on a break. My wife was telling a recent story that had occurred at a grocery store which involved our 4-year-old granddaughter. There had been some conversation about the food in Styrofoam plastic-wrapped containers (pork) between Billie and our granddaughter. Close by, within earshot, an elderly woman announced to our granddaughter that this was pork. But our granddaughter shot back telling the woman that "pork is from a pig and pigs are animals that are alive and don't want to die and that someone had to kill the poor pig to make pork." Billie explained at the water cooler, that the woman had been dumbfounded by the child's detailed response. One practitioner listening to the story said, "She needs to learn respect!" But my wife responded that she didn't feel anything was wrong with the child's outspoken behavior. The other practitioner insisted that "respect" was necessary, thinking this was the crux of the story. Billie explained that our grandchild was just explaining in a truthful manner what pork is and meant no disrespect. As a four year-old she didn't know much about the concept of respect or disrespect as they don't have the filters we tend to learn later in life. She was simply being genuine, open and honest with her feelings and knowledge about pork.

This type of exchange leaves vegans feeling pretty weary. They find themselves in situations where they need to defend themselves or a 4-year-old's innocent compassion in not wanting to kill because when we live in a world where most do not see the killing, respect is more important than pointing out killing. Respect is more important and speaking out for an animal who cannot speak for itself. Respect is more important that speaking out against habits in contradiction displayed by teachers, monks and lay practitioners.

On the contrary, children should be listened to because they speak from their hearts without the cultural bias we all learn. They have not learned to cover up the violent, racist, sexist, and speciesist actions of society, they voice what they see and feel unvarnished by the brush of respect. Nowhere is this more true than the video of Luis Antonio, a 4 year-old Portuguese boy who doesn't want to eat his octopus.[37] You can view the video here: https://www.youtube.com/watch?v=SrU03da2arE

The child advocating for an animal over a human being and the response of respect uncovers this blind spot. Humans are more important than animals. This, of course, is ludicrous from the standpoint of a Buddhist cosmology. We, humans and animals alike, are all connected through karma, dependent origination and the doctrine of emptiness. Indeed, all mother sentient beings are inherently connected. But we are speciesist in our bias. We favor humans without question and without questioning what humans do. This is a blind spot. This is blind spot in our culture and upbringing as well as in our Buddhist communities. Most of us fail to question or even see the carnage going on around us. We ignore change, we fail to get engaged, and we do not speak out. We are comfortable on our cushions practicing patience, generosity, meditation and the middle path with lukewarm numbed dead nerve endings, brain cells, and feelings; clogged with cholesterol, fat, and the adrenal-suffering of those we eat. It is no wonder elementary electrical connections we rely upon to help us function with compassion and wisdom falter and sputter like a cut power line in the aftermath of a storm. We are unable to connect A to B to C when we feed upon the suffering of sentient beings, all the while devastating the earth, our health and spiritual progress.

We live during a great mass murder where 70 billion land animals alone are being killed annually and as a friend David Williams recently wrote about Buddhists, who are vegan:

*"We are like people who might have witnessed human genocide by the Nazis or in Rwanda and who point it out to others with frenzied urgency, feeling that if only people knew the truth they would be aghast at the inhumanity of it and insist that it end; only to find that those people don't want to see and don't want to know; and so the killing goes on, the massacre continues to grow, and we are asked not to scream out loud about it because it is simply 'our belief' and we shouldn't impose it on others ... as if there is some credible alternate belief system where it is okay to do these things to sentient beings; where unleashing our inner barbarian is acceptable; where the three poisons of ignorance, hatred and greed should override our innate feelings of compassion. So the 'curse' of those who are awake to it and who see it clearly is that they can never stop speaking out about it; because to do so would be to deny their practice of the Dharma/Dhamma. I suppose one can quietly abstain, but where is the compassion in that? Is it right action to turn a blind eye to the suffering of other beings?"*

It is not compassionate to turn a blind eye. As vegans we need to always stand our ground because society is so indoctrinated and unseeing. When respect trumps awareness of killing we are eyeless. When respect trumps awareness of killing at a Buddhist retreat, which is based on learning to become "all loving and all compassionate" then the message is not getting through. The compassionate point of view is that of the child who was pointing out that someone had to suffer and die to become food. The child was feeling bad for the packaged body parts in front of her; she wasn't seeing food she was seeing an unfortunate lifeless animal who had wanted life. Respect has nothing to do with the conversation when it's about life and death. But vegans are continually bombarded with derision about their food choices; they are questioned, ridiculed, and laughed at for eating a diet based on not killing--even at Buddhist gatherings.

When I hear stories such as this I find it terribly sad. I find it sad that the simple facts do not suffice for so many non-vegans to see and then change their violent choices. I find it sad that their ability to feel compassion is so limited. I find it sad that their ability to think for themselves is such a struggle. I find it sad that with all the information around them they do not see that non-vegan choices support the continuing suffering of animals through: raping, exploiting, oppressing, enslaving, abusing and murdering. I find it sad that I was just as blind too and I know I must have compassion for all.

# Forgive Me Father For I Have Sinned - The Four Powers

Being raised Catholic I was taught about sin and the powers of confession, how to confess my sins to a priest and to receive a penance of prayers from him to say which would absolve me of any wrong doing. The priest was my get out of jail free card as long as I said my 10 or 20 "Our Fathers and Hail Marys" I was absolved. I could go ahead and do it again and would be absolved again the following week. For whatever reason this never worked for me, I admit I probably didn't understand fully or take it seriously, nor did I ever feel comfortable telling someone else who I had no relationship with my negative thoughts and actions. He was a nameless, faceless being on the other side of a screen, in a closet in which I was sitting or kneeling and I was young. Most of all it was illogical to me as I grew to a young adult with a leaning toward science and reason.

To my surprise in Buddhism I found there is something similar but not quite the same, as a monk cannot absolve another of their negative action. This is because Buddhadharma teaches each of us is responsible for our actions, our own karma. There are no priests to absolve anything negative we might do. In Buddhism we are taught we must change our actions, or change the causes to get different results. We are taught to analyze what we do, understand the causes and conditions for what we do and then use the four powers to purify our negative actions.[38] Cause and result, the interplay of logic and analysis are keys, and understanding is central. It's a very scientific way of looking at life. This logical approach appealed to me since it dealt with cause and effect, cause and result, and changing actions to change the result.

If, as it's said, "confession is good for the soul," -- then it is good to be honest and truthful with oneself. Indeed truth with oneself is at the core of the Buddha's teachings. When he found his fellow ascetics in Deer Park outside of Varanasi, after reaching enlightenment in Bodhgaya it is said his first teaching was on the Four Noble Truths, the truth of suffering, the truth of the cause of suffering, the truth that suffering can be eliminated and the truth of the path to eliminate suffering. Two sets of results with their requisite causes. Finding truth is core to the teachings of the Buddha.

We kill sentient beings by living, by the mere act of being alive. This is part of the First Noble Truth, the truth of suffering in Samsara and there is nothing we can do about it at one level of examination since it is unavoidable. When I walk I am sure I am killing sentient beings. When I drive my car I am killing sentient beings. When I eat organic green peas purchased from grocery frozen section, I know that somewhere in the cultivation process, the tilling of the soil, the growing, picking, packaging, and shipping, sentient beings are being killed. I regret that deeply. I regret that my living causes death and suffering. But what can be done? How can this be rectified? And while we kill inadvertently as a by-product of life, to not-kill is also central to Buddhism. As defined in the First Precept found in the Mahayana Brahmajala Sutra:

*"A disciple of the Buddha shall not himself kill, encourage others to kill, kill by expedient means, praise killing, rejoice at witnessing killing, or kill through incantation or deviant mantras. He*

*must not create the causes, conditions, methods, or karma of killing, and shall not intentionally kill any living creature.*

*"As a Buddha's disciple, he ought to nurture a mind of compassion and filial piety, always devising expedient means to rescue and protect all beings. If instead, he fails to restrain himself and kills sentient beings without mercy, he commits a major offense."* [39]

I would argue that while the inadvertent death of some sentient beings is unavoidable, there are "avoidable deaths" we can commit to stop being a part of, i.e. there are two types of killing: those we cannot stop from happening and those we can. Killing of insects through cultivation of crops is unavoidable as is killing that occurs when walking or even breathing. Eating meat is a type of killing which is completely avoidable. However, both types of killing (as should all negativities) be purified using the four powers. The unavoidable type takes more of the prayer form of the four powers while that avoidable type of killing takes more of an action type of the form of the four powers.

If I kill and can stop killing (avoidable type of killing) then I should stop killing when I realize that action is avoidable. Furthermore, I can use the four powers to purify the negative karma I have received for killing. In general the four powers work like this: I look at my situation/my life, I become truthful about it, I acknowledge the truth of the situation, I find something I regret, I renounce it, I resolve to not do it again, I take antidote action to remedy it, and I take refuge in the enlightened society to help me and support me in the change.

How do you make up for killing and hurting sentient beings? What is hurting? And to whom will you make it up? Gelek Rimpoche states in Odyssey to Freedom:

*"Well, I will do something to make it up. To whom? Oh, whomever I have hurt. You know what negativity truly is? Hurting other beings. Almost all negativities are violence. Buddha always said, 'If you are following me, don't hurt other people. Hurting and causing hurt to other people is not dharma practice.' The true negativity is causing pain for others, hurting beings, including yourself, too. That is the real true negativity."[40]*

Hurting is negative and hurting is violence. Hurting is also not dharma practice. To make up for killing and hurting sentient beings we enact the four powers, but how can the four powers relate to eating animals? We simply meditate on each of the four points; regret, resolution, remedy, and refuge and take appropriate action.

# Regret

We review our actions of eating sentient beings and the impact it has on the animals, ourselves and the planet. We understand and acknowledge the immense suffering animals have on factory farms, on hooks and nets at sea, upon the ships at sea when pulled from the ocean, and at slaughterhouses. We witness the suffering of humans who eat them and realize the disease states that eating animal products, eating sentient beings support in ourselves and others. We regret our support of the market for animal products and its effect on global warming, usage of resources, and pollution of land, air, and water. We feel intense regret for all these conditions for which we have been a cause and we renounce this activity.

# Resolution

We resolve to never do this again. We resolve to never again be the cause for sentient beings, considered as food by a human culture which embraces structural violence, to suffer, become imprisoned, have intense fear, misery, and pain on our behalf. We resolve to remove ourselves from this violence and negativity and our resolution takes the form of becoming vegan for the benefit of all sentient beings.

# Remedy

We decide to take antidote action, we become "engaged" Buddhists. We look up the 30-day vegan pledge; we prepare ourselves by clearing out our refrigerator and pantry of all animal products. We stock up on vegan cruelty-free products and arm ourselves with a large number of recipes. Additionally, we resolve to lead everyone to veganism, as Bodhisattva's in training since we are going to free all sentient beings, this also includes all the animals in the oceans and in factory farms. By doing this we re-direct the cause and effect and our karma changes.

# Refuge

Lastly, as Buddhist practitioners we take refuge in prayer form to all enlightened society, all Buddhas and Bodhisattvas. We confess our actions, regret our actions, resolve to change our actions and remedy our actions. Buddhas and Bodhisattvas become witnesses and we rely on their awakened minds to help us with our decision. When we meditate on this we believe it is happening. We also take refuge in our Sangha members, those on the same path of non-violence: Vegan Society. We participate in blogs, join organizations, meet people and participate in education for others.

By taking these four steps we change our behavior and it is said we purify the negative karma and gain merit, i.e. positive karma. In this manner we have made something that is deemed permanent, karma for doing something bad, into karma for doing something good and what we did that was bad is erased. Karma after all is impermanent as long as you are making needed change, regret the action, and are truthfully honest about it. Indeed the best antidote action for supporting the killing of beings used for food is to just stop eating them. When we stop eating beings, the market for their bodies and secretions (milk and cheese) will end.

The question is: can the negative karma of eating sentient beings, causing harm to the planet, and my own body in reality be purified? In Buddhism the answer is yes because all things are impermanent, even karma. Just make the change and stop waiting for the negative consequences to take place. I was taught that while karma is definite, it will happen, and generally it will happen quickly, it is also taught that it is changeable, it is impermanent. Even Angulimala who killed 999 people during the Buddha's time purified himself and became an ordained monk. So if you can purify something, change your action and thus change your result, why not do it?

According to Gelek Rimpoche,

*"Since things are purifyable, why don't you purify? Why are you waiting for the consequences to take place? It is the same for any illness that we have. If we detect or diagnose any illness that we have early enough, we can treat it and get better. Why do we have to wait until it becomes too late? The same thing here. The negativities are going to give us terrible results, so why don't we purify them long before they come in?"*[41]

Becoming vegan and helping others become vegan is one of the easiest and best usages of the four powers because it is a form of engaged Buddhism, it gives you something to act upon that is concrete and has immediate results for your own health, the well-being of sentient beings and the ecology of the planet. It fights structural violence instantly by bringing to a halt your compliance with it.

As such, going vegan is purifying negative actions. As negative action obscures our own Buddha nature and the ability to see reality as it is, this action of going vegan helps us along the path. When we rid ourselves of the negativity involved in the killing of suffering beings and rid our bodies of the flesh filled with the hormones of misery and secretions of despair we become more compassionate, open, and free. We become more Buddha-like and this pushes us another step along the path to eventual full awakening.

# What Were the Effects of Veganism on My Meditation Practice?

I began formal daily meditation in January 1997, shortly after meeting Gelek Rimpoche at the Unitarian Church on Woodward in Birmingham, Michigan. His teaching was a general talk on Tibetan Buddhism, karma and reincarnation. I decided to stop wasting time and begin sitting there and then. Meditation is difficult. Trying to still one's mind from going hither and thither is nearly impossible. It takes many years of calm guidance, watching, and gentle effort to begin to realize moments of true clarity. For those of you on this path to attempting to "tame" your mind I would like to suggest that going vegan is a very helpful step. I personally have experienced some positive incremental improvements which I believe may be due to the diet change. I have increased energy and clarity from the diet and this helps when sitting and trying to keep my focus. When it comes to meditation, it is taught that human beings have two general categories of mind, wandering mind or sinking mind. We either have a tendency toward one or the other. I personally tend to have a sinking mind rather than an agitated mind, a mind that can easily fall asleep and so having more energy and being clearer in my visualizations is beneficial.

As discussed, just prior to becoming vegan I was fully an omnivore eating a Standard American Diet (SAD) high in factory farmed products of beef, chicken, pork, fish, eggs and cheese. I ate at a minimum one meat product per meal. Eating all this meat was making me obese and clogging my arteries. For my height, my weight was too heavy -- 40 pounds too heavy and my BMI was terrible. Losing weight has been very helpful but I also think there are other factors such as clearer ethical conscience, value-alignment, a reduction of hormones, pesticides, vermicides, herbicides and animal adrenaline within my body that has also helped me observe an incremental change.

As part of the Standard American Diet I ate, I was a getting natural and unnatural hormones of the bovine species with every bite of cheese I ate. I was eating all the other hormones from the bovine species as cows are milked while they are pregnant for eight of their nine month gestation period, a standard industry practice. These are hormones not made by my human body. These were things I was adding to my body that I am sure I did not need to survive, things foreign (not present in my mother's milk) which I am sure my body was expending energy to eliminate, neutralize, and counteract in some manner. Nature and natural selection designed cow's milk for baby cows not for human adults.

As part of the standard American diet I was getting my daily dosage of pesticides from the residue left over in the feed that the animals ate[42], whose fat I ate in meat and drank in milk, and whose fat created fat on me. Animals produced by modern agribusiness in the U.S. and elsewhere are fed conventionally grown plants and grain which have residues of the pesticides and herbicides used to grow the crops. With every bite I was a getting my daily dosage of these man-made compounds, which again were counterproductive for health and foreign to my body which had to expend energy to eliminate and neutralize their effects. My body does not need herbicides, from the

GMO soy and corn fed to the animals I ate, nor the arsenic found in chickens. [43]

As part of the Standard American Diet I was getting my daily dosage of animal adrenalin due to their terror and misery, which is excreted during the petrifying and brutal trip to the slaughterhouse and the actual slaughter on the killing floor--the scene of millions of murders daily. Animals are not dumb as we would like to believe, regardless of what some may declare. Animals experience great fear and suffer with the dread of impending death for themselves and for their fellow beings who they hear and smell dying. Animals want to escape while being violently funneled into the killing area. Remember the stories of cows who have escaped slaughter and we all reveled in their good fortune to escape? [44] This is true for chickens, cows, pigs and all other animals. One can find many photos and videos of animals going to slaughter, or in the killing room on the internet. They are not happy. You can see they are afraid. You can see they are trying to escape. [45]

Many cultures like the taste of excessive adrenalin in their meat. The Chinese boil dogs alive torturing them in painful deaths to create meat that has more, rather than less, adrenaline in the body at death. When we are very afraid for our lives we excrete adrenaline hormones are part of our fight or flight response. Animals do this too. Those of us who eat animals are eating the adrenaline from these scared animals. Every day I was getting my daily doses of fear, misery and terror in the bodies of the innocent sentient beings I was eating. Nowhere have I heard in the teachings of the Buddha that the eating of fear, misery and terror located in a sentient being's dead body are beneficial to one's meditation practice.

Going vegan and tending toward organic grain, fruit and vegetables I have eliminated: antibiotics, growth hormones, pregnancy hormones, herbicides, pesticides, animal adrenaline, urea, cholesterol, excess protein, and fat.

All of these changes I believe had had a positive effect on my body and mind connection. I do believe I am functioning noticeably clearer because my body does not have to deal with these pernicious substances any longer. My blood vessels are cleaner and clearer as witnessed by my lower cholesterol levels and triglyceride levels. My sugar levels are normal. My blood pressure is normal. I am on no prescription medications. My conscience is clearer too - I am not impacting global hunger any longer and my carbon footprint has decreased dramatically. I am helping people, the planet, and myself—as my morals and ethics are allied with my eating habits this has allowed my outer being to be more aligned with my inner being. With everything flowing clearer in my blood I believe I have more sensitivity and am able to empathize better, have more responsibility, and feel more vibrant and alive. While I have not fully subdued my mind, anger, attachment, lust, guilt, greed jealousy, narcissism, and other negative emotions, I do believe I am calmer, more peaceful, and less aggressive. Perhaps I am mentally a little more stable. I certainly have greater compassion. I attribute this to the body mind connection and my detoxification. There is no doubt a certain amount of toxicity in the eating of animal bodies we are accustomed to ingesting. I no longer need to have denial about what I am eating. I can fully look at my food and have no regret. I no longer have adrenaline entering my body from the sorrow of a being who wanted to live rather than die. I no longer have the sorrow of a mother hen in a battery cage watching her egg roll down a tube away from her, or the sorrow and adrenaline from a mother cow who has just witnessed her calf taken from her causing her to bellow in agony for up to two weeks. I think these are all factors in my increased mental stability, clarity and peace.

Due to this change, the electrical connections at a chemical level seem to be working better; my synapses are ostensibly more open, healthier and natural. I am more the true person I was destined and genetically evolved to become, and there seems to be scientific evidence to support fact that the same diet that helps our body also helps our brain, as new studies using PET scans is showing relationship between cholesterol and Alzheimer's dementia. There is a lot of evidence indicating that Alzheimer's disease is primarily a vascular disorder and thus what is bad for our heart muscle is bad for the brain.[46]

I make no claim to any enlightenment whatsoever, or to any special illumination, or insight; no claim to being able to sit in Samadhi for more than a fleeting moment; and no claim to having tamed my mind. But being vegan and sitting on my cushion with my hand on the Earth I am witnessing in a calmer space, with greater clarity, more peace, and connectivity with the world and my relationship to the world (and all the beings in it) with greater compassion than I ever have, and so for me this has been helpful along the my path. This is a tremendous gift to receive, just by changing my diet. When one stops eating beings one realizes at a deeper level every being is the same as you.

# No Superiority Just Happiness, Hopefulness, Humbleness, and Helpfulness

The infliction of pain and suffering on animals is not the big image I keep in front of me. What I envision is a vegan world of compassionate living, a world full of happiness, hopefulness, humbleness and helpfulness. As Buddhists we all agree that not-committing any type of violence against human beings or non-human beings (animals) is a better way to live one's life. It's a pretty simple thing to agree upon and from a moral and ethical standpoint the practice of ahimsa is superior because of the good karma it creates.

Being vegan is very similar to living this ethic of ahimsa in one's daily life. It's not an end in-and-of-itself, but a process. Being vegan is simply another path, just another road to travel as a means to an end; it can be a way to become more mindful, more compassionate and help align one's values of not harming. Personally, I am humbled to be a vegan. I am so thankful to my daughter and wife for challenging me to change my tastes. I am thankful for all the teachers in my life who have shown me that it is good to be open to change. I am not superior to anyone as a vegan. How could I be? I was an eater of meat, fish and dairy not long ago. I spent the better part of my life eating animals. When I ate animals I didn't look deeply at what was on my plate. I didn't make the connection. I made excuses like everyone else. I am so grateful to those heroes, whom I have learned from, by whom I was able to gain knowledge, awareness, and turn myself toward love and compassion. I am humbled rather than feeling any sort of superiority.

I don't feel ethically superior or morally superior to those who still eat animals, I only feel deep sorrow for all the animals living in captivity and dying in slaughterhouses. I feel deep sorrow for the humans inflicting the suffering upon these animals. I feel deep sorrow for the planet being scarred. But what keeps me from spiraling into nihilism is the big picture view I have of a vegan world, sustainable, compassionate and full of love and knowing that if I can change my habits, anyone can.

# You and Saka Dawa

And so we come to the last subject in this book, YOU, and what you will do, or have done, with the information offered. Will you hold onto the culturally learned ways of thinking, feeling and acting toward animal food? Or will you decide to change to a kind, more compassionate vegan lifestyle? As you have read this book, have you thought about taking the 30-day vegan challenge yourself?

The world has changed immensely since the Buddha walked the Ganges river plain 2,600 years ago. Around the Buddha's time there were approximately thirty to fifty million human beings on the planet[47]. In 1812, we reached the 1,000 million (one billion) mark. By 1912, the number had jumped up fifty percent to 1,500 million people but in 2012 we reached the 7,000 million (seven billion) people milestone. Today's seven billion people act as though it is 1812 or 1912 in many ways but most tragically in how we relate to animals as food, entertainment, clothing and test subjects. This cultural baggage rides almost inconspicuously with us but it impacts our world in devastating ways. A few environmental data points help to bear this out.

We take 2.7 TRILLION lives out of our oceans each year for food consumption. It has been calculated our oceans will be lifeless by 2048 unless we stop eating sea food as three-fourths of global fisheries are exhausted or depleted. 650,000 innocent bystanders, whales and dolphins, are killed each year by our fishing fleets and for every 1 pound of fish captured up to 5 pounds of bycatch (unintended sea life) are entrapped and killed. All these billions and trillions of beings suffer and die to be on our plates. As they suffer and die, we will also suffer and die.

On land we domesticate and slaughter 70 BILLION animals per year[48] to feed our voracious appetite for flesh food and as a consequence produce more greenhouse gas than all the combined cars, trucks, buses, trains, and ships in the world. Cows produce 150 billion gallons of methane daily[49] which is 25 – 100 times more destructive than Co2. Frighteningly, one to two acres of forest are cleared every second to grow feed, for beef cattle.[50] The cost is staggering, for our ability and choice, to eat meat. Livestock animals now cover 45% of the earth's total land surface[51] and have been the cause of destruction of 136 million rainforest acres. Our attachment to eating animals is the leading cause of species extinction, dead zones in our oceans, wildlife habitat destruction, and water pollution. While fracking utilizes between 70 to 140 billion gallons of water per year, animal agriculture uses between 34 and 76 TRILLION gallons annually. We lament fossil fuel company' agendas to find and produce more oil but fail to recognize our central part in this catastrophe, the being at the end of our forks. In addition animal agriculture, whose ecological footprint is responsible for more greenhouse gas emissions than all global transport combined, is expected to rise 80% by 2050 to feed our need and demand for flesh. Today fifty-one percent of all greenhouse gas emissions can be traced back to one cause – animal agriculture (animals and the food we grow to feed them). At today's unsustainable pace six million animals are killed every hour for food, and yet the animal agriculture and fishing industries can't keep up with our demand for meat and other animal products.

And so with this data in mind, and the untold suffering that goes along with it, we should realize a change is needed for us all to practice more generosity and compassion toward animals, the earth and ourselves. This is reminiscent of Saka Dawa and its relationship to veganism.

## Saka Dawa – 30-Days of Merit

In our sangha it is known as Saka Dawa,[52] but in many other Buddhist communities it is known as Wesak or Vesak. "Saka" is the name of a star that appears in the fourth lunar month of the Tibetan calendar, and "Dawa" means month. Whatever one calls it, it is a month (generally falling in May or June) where Buddhists around the world commemorate Buddha Shakyamuni's birth, enlightenment and paranirvana (death). It is believed that the merit from positive activities generated during this month is multiplied many-thousand fold. As an example, saving one animal's life during this time, is like saving 100,000 animals, and so it is also known as the month of merits.

There is one day during this month, the 15th day of the full moon that is considered the most auspicious. On that particular day many practitioners take a pledge of observing the eight Mahayana Precepts as a 24-hour commitment. It is said that relying on the eight Mahayana Precepts, even for the short 24-hour period, has tremendous benefit. Along with the precepts, is a commitment to fast from 12 noon until the following sunrise. One meal is allowed prior to noon but it must be a vegetarian meal.

Everyone meets prior to sunrise at about 5:30 am and while it is still dark outside prayers are recited, a short mandala offering is made, and then one makes a commitment to follow the eight precepts. The first five of the precepts are the same as have been discussed earlier: do not kill, do not steal, do not lie, do engage in sexual activity and do not use intoxicants. The additional three are:

- avoid eating more than one meal,
- do not sit on large expensive beds with pride, and avoid sitting on animals skins,
- do not adorn yourself with perfume, rosaries or other jewelry and avoid singing, dancing and playing music

The 24-hour vows are taken to bring our attention to our actions and thus avoid specific negative activities. They are an ethical mindfulness exercise. During our 24-hour commitment some good actions are commonly identified which one should take part in and make an effort to do. This is all in an attempt to accumulate merit during this this auspicious time. Some examples are:

- Be generous to the animals and abstain from eating any meat (for the day or the month)
- Be generous and contribute to monasteries and to individual monks and nuns
- Recite mantras
- Visit holy sites and make prostrations around holy places
- Be generous by giving alms and money to beggars
- Purchase animals, such as fish, which are to be killed and then liberate them

By abstaining from eating meat and freeing animals that are going to be slaughtered some of what Saka Dawa purports dovetails into what vegans do. If refraining from eating meat, freeing animals, and not using animal skins are merit gaining activities, then vegans participate in merit gaining activities every single day of the year. Vegans seek to exclude, as far as possible, all forms of exploitation and cruelty to animals for food, clothing, entertainment, and cosmetics/drugs.[53] Furthermore, vegans promote alternatives for the benefit of animals, people and the environment. For a vegan abstaining from eating meat is an everyday occurrence. Their practice of not eating, using, or purchasing any products that are used by animals has the secondary effect of having less animals brought into life and then killed. No fur, no cosmetics, no leather. Additional secondary effects of a vegan diet result in vegans contributing less to global environmental destruction and making natural resources available to be used by others. Vegans use far less natural resources than omnivores, carnivores and vegetarians and this can be viewed as a generous action.

Taking this one step further it would be an act of generosity to take the 30-day vegan challenge during Saka Dawa. What better way to create merit, when the benefits of virtuous acts are multiplied thousands and millions of times? According to the Vegan Calculator[54] by simply eating vegan for 30-days you would save: 30 animal's lives, 33,000 gallons of water, 1,200 pounds of grain, 900 square feet of forest, and 600 lbs. of Co2. If you made this commitment for the rest of your life just think what merit you could accrue? As a vegan, for five and one-half years, I have saved: 2,005 animals' lives, 2,205,500 gallons of water, 80,200 lbs. of grain, 60,150 square feet of forest, and 40,100 lbs. of Co2.

http://thevegancalculator.com/#calculator

Being vegan is about reducing suffering. Being a Buddhist is about reducing suffering, ours and all sentient beings. Wouldn't it be wonderful if Buddhists around the world would prepare to become vegans in 2016 by committing to the 30-day vegan challenge and making this commitment at dawn on Saka Dawa day. By doing this for one-month during Saka Dawa month great merit, great changes in one's awareness, and great changes in one's tastebuds would be produced. Each and every practitioner would save the lives of 30 animals. And so I leave you with this idea: Go Vegan for Saka Dawa!

In the end only you can change what is at the end of your fork. The choice is up to you.

http://www.the30dayveganchallenge.com

http://www.pcrm.org/kickstartHome

# Dedication and Thanks

I want to thank my root teacher, Gelek Rimpoche, from the bottom of my heart and express my sincere gratitude. I have spent countless hours in retreats with him for the past eighteen years and he has tried to pass to me what little my mind can understand of the precious teachings coming from Tibet on Buddhism. Gelek Rimpoche is the founder of Jewel Heart, a Tibetan Buddhist learning center with chapters around the world, including of all places Ann Arbor, Michigan.

I dedicate this book to my wife Billie, who has supported my efforts to be a better person all these years, who supported this crazy idea to write about veganism and Buddhism, who has been by my soul mate and at my side for thirty-eight years of marriage. In all my craziness, childishness, and ego grasping she has always sustained my efforts to improve. She generously praises me for my qualities and fearlessly points out my faults and helping me become increasingly more the person I would like to be however difficult this is in attaining. And she challenged me to take the 30-day vegan pledge. Thank you my love.

Thank you to my daughters, Stephanie and Cristina, who courageously brought the plight of animals to the forefront of our family and generously helped in multiple readings and editing of this manuscript -- even when school workloads were heavy. I love and appreciate you both so much.

And a big thanks to Elizabeth Hurwitz, who read drafts of this manuscript, made suggestions, and was always so very positive about this endeavor – thanks for being a shining light my friend!

Lastly I dedicate this book to many of the animal advocates and activists I have met on Facebook, especially those whose interests are similar to my own (Buddhism and Veganism): Tashi Nyima, David Williams, and all the other members of the two groups: "*Vegans – On the Bodhisattva Path*", and "*Ahimsayana – The Way of the Vegan Buddhist*". The members of these two groups are enthusiastic, compassionate, and tireless in the sharing of information, asking questions and civil discussion. Thanks for the inspiration.

If just one animal's life has become spared by someone skipping a meal of meat, fish, dairy and eggs then this book has been worth the time and effort spent writing and publishing it. If someone's health improves due to a diet change, this effort has been worthwhile. If less environmental destruction is witnessed due to changes in anyone's eating habits, this effort has been worthwhile. I dedicate any merit from this book to benefit all sentient beings may they be free from suffering and may they dwell in equanimity, happy, and at peace.

# Thanks for Reading This Book

If you liked this book please leave an honest review on Amazon.

Please feel free to reach out to me with comments, suggestions and questions at John.Bussineau@gmail.com

# Expand Your Knowledge

There are endless sources today to understand the plight of animals, the planet and our health. Listed below are a few sources I highly recommend:

Take the Vegan Challenge
- The 30-day Vegan Challenge:

  http://www.the30dayveganchallenge.com

- The 21-day Kickstart:

  http://www.pcrm.org/kickstartHome

Books
- The World Peace Diet by Dr. Will Tuttle
- The Great Compassion by Norm Phelps
- The China Study by T. Colin Campbell and Thomas M. Campbell II
- Eating Animals by Jonathan Safran Foer
- Breaking the Food Seduction by Neal Barnard, M.D.
- Why We Love Dogs, Eat Pigs, and Wear Cows by Melanie Joy
- Slaughterhouse by Gail Eisnitz
- Eternal Treblinka by Charles Patterson
- The Food Revolution by John Robbins
- Meatonomics by David Robinson Simon

Movies
- Animals and The Buddha: http://tinyurl.com/og4akxv
- Cowspiracy: http://www.cowspiracy.com/
- Earthlings: https://www.youtube.com/watch?v=ibuQ-J04eLQ
- Forks Over Knives: http://www.forksoverknives.com/
- Vegucated: http://www.getvegucated.com/
- Blackfish: http://www.blackfishmovie.com/

Organizations
- Dharma Voices for Animals: http://dharmavoicesforanimals.org/
- Mercy for Animals: http://www.mercyforanimals.org/
- Compassion Over Killing: http://cok.net/
- Peta: http://www.peta.org/
- Farm Sanctuary: http://www.farmsanctuary.org/
- Physicians Committee for Responsible Medicine: http://www.pcrm.org/

Websites and Face Book Groups

- The World Peace Diet: Dr. Will Tuttle: http://www.worldpeacediet.com/
- Nutrition Facts: Michael Greger, M.D.: http://nutritionfacts.org/

- Tashi Nyima, The Great Middle Way:
  https://greatmiddleway.wordpress.com/
- Vegans – On the Bodhisattva Path:
  http://tinyurl.com/votbp
- Ahimsayana Buddhism – The Way of Vegan
  Buddhists: http://tinyurl.com/abwotvb
- Bearing Witness, Toronto Pig Save:
  https://www.facebook.com/groups/144171365
  639268/

# Glossary

Ahimsa – a principle from Buddhist, Hindu and Jain background that informs followers to do no harm to any sentient being.

Analytical Meditation – a form of meditation practice based upon study, reflection, and logical inquiry. It is founded on reasons, arguments, and conclusions.

Angulimala – an infamous ruthless serial killer who lived during the Buddha's time. The name literally means finger necklace, as he would cut a finger from each of his victim's hands and string it onto a necklace he wore.

Atisha Dipamkara – (982-1055) A great Indian scholar who spent the last seventeen years of his life in Tibet, conveying many significant teachings. He is celebrated for his short dissertation call the Light on the Path to Enlightenment, a concise route to enlightenment which became the Lam Rim. The followers of Atisha became known as the Kadampa school.

Bodhimind – In Sanskrit the term is Bodhichitta or Bodhicitta. It defines the altruistic motivation of a Bodhisattva and is a mind that is directed towards the attainment of Buddhahood, for the sake of all living beings. A person with Bodhimind has a fully opened heart dedicated to delivering all beings from suffering.

Bodhisattva – Is a living being who has generated the commitment to attain enlightenment for the sake of all living beings. The term Bodhisattva refers to those on many levels: from those who have generated the aspiration to become enlightened for the first time to those who have actually entered the Bodhisattva path, which is developed through the ten stages (called bhumis) and culminates in enlightenment, the attainment of Buddhahood.

Carnism — A term coined by Melanie Joy, from www.carnism.org: "Carnism is the invisible belief system, or ideology, that conditions people to eat certain animals. Carnism is essentially the opposite of veganism; "carn" means "flesh" or "of the flesh" and "ism" denotes a belief system. Most people view eating animals as a given, rather than a choice; in meat-eating cultures around the world people typically don't think about why they find the flesh of some animals disgusting and the flesh of other animals appetizing, or why they eat any animals at all. But when eating animals is not a necessity for survival, as is the case in much of the world today, it is a choice - and choices always stem from beliefs." Also see Melanie Joy.

Casomorphin - are a peptide or protein fragment, which comes from the digestion of milk protein. Casein makes up 80% of the protein substance found in cow's milk. Casein has been shown to breakdown in our stomach producing the peptide, casomorphin. One of the peculiar properties of casomorphin is that it has an opioid effect on our body.

Concentrated Meditation — is called Shamatha or Samatha in Sanskrit and Zhi Nay in Tibetan. Zhi means "pacified, peace," and nay is "remains." So, zhi nay is about pacifying all difficulties, obstacles and imbalances (wandering and sinking) within your mind and reaching, maintaining and remaining in a state of tranquility, mental calm. One can feel they are really getting somewhere when we can train our minds to stay on the object of meditation for a 20 minute timeframe without wandering off or sinking into drowsiness.

Factory Farming – Factory farms are where almost all (95%) of animal-derived food comes from in U.S.; they dominate food production. They as also called CAFO, Confined Area Feeding Operations, and by their very nature employ abusive practices that maximize profits generally at the expense of the environment, communities, animal welfare, and human health. They are neither idyllic nor spacious pasture-like accommodations that we may imagine, but rather places of extreme confinement where animals are regarded as commodities rather than living beings. There are numerous practices used where animals are mutilated and bred to grow unnaturally quick to maximize profit. Factory farms put a huge strain upon the environment due to so many animals in one place which causes pollution of our land, water and air. There are many challenges to animals' health on factory farms and this is augmented by the usage of antibiotics, however, this use also creates a perfect breeding ground for drug-resistant bacteria like MSRA to reproduce.

Four Noble Truths – 1) the truth of suffering (it exists); 2) the cause of suffering (ignorance, attachment and aversion); 3) the is a way out (Nirvana); 4) there is a path to follow to get out (Dharma)

Khedrup Je - (1385-1438) The younger of Tsongkhapa's two heart disciples. He was a vegetarian and believed all who have taken the Bodhisattva vow should abstain from meat eating. This belief was for all monks, nuns and lay who practice the Mahayana. See www.Shabkar.org for more information.

Lam Rim - the literal translation is: 'stages on the path'. This form of Buddhist practice was brought to Tibet from India by Atisha Dīpaṃkara in 1042. The stages refer to various steps in in the spiritual path to enlightenment. Gelek Rimpoche has taught a version of this called the 'Odyssey to Freedom' since 1997 where 64-steps are examined.

Mahayana – is the so-called "great vehicle" as it transports all sentient beings to enlightenment or Buddhahood. It is distinguished from Theravada, which focuses on personal liberation. The basis of the Mahayana path is great compassion; and its aim, rather than personal nirvana, is to become fully a Buddha in order to help all sentient life become fully awakened and free no matter how long this takes, lifetime after lifetime.

Meditation - The process of guiding, training and transmuting the mind that leads one to enlightenment. The process of becoming thoroughly familiar with positive attitudes and accurate perspectives through both analytical investigation and single-pointed concentration.

Melanie Joy Ph.D. - Melanie Joy, Ph.D., Ed.M. is a Harvard-educated psychologist, professor of psychology and sociology at the University of Massachusetts Boston. She is a celebrated speaker and the author of the award-winning book <u>Why We Love Dogs, Eat Pigs, and Wear Cows</u>.

Milarepa – (1040-1123) A Tibetan yogi who achieved Buddhahood in one lifetime. His biography is a an example of hardship undertaken in order to attain enlightenment. He was the student of Marpa and a vegetarian.

Sadhana – a spiritual practice or discipline which leads to perfecting oneself.

Samadhi – Is the meditative power of mind that has the ability to concentrate single-pointedly totally absorbing one's mind in an object of concentration. It is a state of profound meditative absorption; single-pointed concentration on the actual nature of things, completely free from rambling thought and dualistic perceptions.
Sangha - a Buddhist community of monks, nuns, novices, and laity.

Sentient Being – a being who has feelings, wants, desires, who can experience pleasure and pain, and can suffer.

Shabkar Tsodruk Rangdrol - (1781-1851) A great Tibetan yogi who advocated for the ideals of vegetarianism.
Sinking Mind – the opposite of wandering mind this is the other common obstacle we all fall into and must learn to work with and through to gain a stable lucid meditation state. Sinking mind is characterized by drowsiness, heaviness, a dimming of your awareness, up to actually falling asleep. Two antidotes used to combat sinking mind are to simply sit up straighter and to open your eyes.

Six Paramitas - The six paramitas (perfections in Sanskrit) are: 1) generosity or giving (dana in Sanskrit); 2) morality or ethical discipline (sila in Sanskrit); 3) tolerance or patience or forbearance (ksanti in Sanskrit); 4) diligence, joyous perseverance or enthusiasm (virya in Sanskrit); meditation or concentration (dhyana in Sanskrit) and; 6) wisdom (prajna in Sanskrit).

Speciesism - is a predisposition and bias that the interests of members of one's own species supersede the interests of members of other species. That humans are special and deserve special status over other species can be found in many religious texts but not in Buddhism, whose interest is in the eventual enlightenment of all sentient beings. To assign different values, rights or special consideration to individual sentient beings solely on the basis of their species is against Buddhists tenets. As an example, in the United States dogs and cats have more rights and value as individuals than do pigs, chickens and cows. Dogs and cats are pets and family members. It's ok to eat pigs, chickens and cows but if you murder your dog or cat in your backyard and put them on the barbeque you could be charged with cruelty and certainly you may not have many neighbors coming over for dinner. However in China, dog and cat meat is normal food. If we find the eating of cats and dogs abhorrent, but not the eating of pigs, chickens and cows, we may have a speciesist blind spot. This term is also related and similar to racism and sexism.

Spent Cow – A spent dairy cow is one whose production has fallen below accepted levels of productivity and profitability; as such, it also denotes dairy cow that cannot become pregnant again. When a dairy cow cannot become pregnant her milk dries up. Spent dairy cows go to slaughter just as all other beef animals.

T. Colin Campbell - Dr. T. Colin Campbell has been at the forefront of nutrition research for over 40 years. His legacy, the China Project, is the most comprehensive study of health and nutrition ever conducted. Dr. Campbell is a professor Emeritus at Cornell University and is most well-known for co-authoring the bestselling book The China Study with his son, Thomas Campbell, MD. Dr. Campbell's expertise and scientific interests encompass relationships between diet and diseases, particularly the causation of cancer. He has focused on nutritional status and long term health. Surprisingly, Campbell started his life on a dairy farm, but is now widely-known for researching links between animal-based protein diets and disease. For more on Dr. T. Colin Campbell visit: http://nutritionstudies.org/about/board/dr-t-colin-campbell/

Tsongkhapa – (1357-1419) a great fourteenth-century scholar and teacher who reformed the Kadampa tradition and founded the Gelug branch of Tibetan Buddhism. He was a prolific author and finalized the work begun by Atisha, writing several Lamrims, the most well-known being the Great exposition on the Stages of the Path, Lamrim Chenmo. He is regarded a full enlightened being.

Veganism - a way of life which seeks to eliminate, as far as is possible and practicable, all forms of exploitation of, and cruelty to, animals for food, clothing or any other purpose. Veganism is not a destination but something to perfect and improve upon as we live our lives. One very important component of veganism is the reduction of suffering in the world today. Vegans try lessening suffering and working for animal liberation, realizing perfection, while fleeting is to be strived for.

Wandering Mind – the normal state of mind most of us have which travels all over the place regularly landing onto things we are attached to when we sit and try meditate and focus. This state of mind is also called excitation or busy mind. In Zhi Nay (Tibetan) or Shamatha (Pali/Sanskrit), meditation we train the mind to be able to focus and concentrate by practicing single-pointed meditation, in many traditions this starts as mindfulness of breathing.

# The Buddha, The Vegan and You: Parts II, III, and IV

To be published in the near future:

**The Buddha, The Vegan and You, Part II:**
The Meat Delusion, How to Become Healthier and Save the Environment

**The Buddha, The Vegan and You, Part III:**
Sentient and the Suffering, the Living Hell of Pigs, Chickens and Dairy Cows

**The Buddha, The Vegan and You, Part IV:**
Bodhisattvas Are Vegan

# Notes

[1] *Kyabje Gelek Rimpoche* is the founder of Jewel Heart Tibetan Learning Center. Jewel Heart is dedicated to the preservation of Tibetan Buddhism and to bringing the practice of this rich tradition within the context of contemporary life to everyone. Gelek Rimpoche established his first Western teaching center in Nijmegen, Netherlands, in 1985. In 1988, Jewel Heart was founded as a non-profit organization in Ann Arbor, Michigan, with chapters and study groups throughout the US, in Malaysia and Singapore and the Netherlands.

[2] Tsoknyi Rinpoche. *Four Thoughts that Turn the Mind to the Dharma*. Accessed May 2015. http://www.tsoknyirinpoche.org/2575/web-teaching-i-2/

Drepung Gomang Monastery. *The Four Foundations: thoughts which turn the mind towards the dharma*. Accessed May 2015. http://drepunggomang.org/dharma-topics/123-the-four-foundations-thoughts-which-turn-the-mind-towards-the-dharma

[3] Casomorphin Sources

Barnard N. (2003) Opiates on a Cracker: The Cheese Seduction. In Barnard, *Breaking the Food Seduction* (pp. 49-60). New York, NY: St. Martins Press

Aslam M. & Hurley W. August 5, 1998. *Biological Activities of Peptides Derived from Milk Proteins*. Accessed October 2015 from http://livestocktrail.illinois.edu/dairynet/paperDisplay.cfm?ContentID=249

Danovich T. March 16, 2015. *If You're Basically Addicted to Cheese, There Could Be a Good Reason Why*. Accessed, May 2015, from http://mic.com/articles/112656/if-you-re-basically-addicted-to-cheese-there-could-be-a-good-reason-why

Harris J. October 22, 2015. *Cheese really is crack. Study reveals cheese is as addictive as drugs.* Accessed, October 2015, from
http://www.latimes.com/food/dailydish/la-dd-cheese-addictive-drugs-20151022-story.html

US National Library of Medicine. National Institutes of Health. Accessed October 2015
http://www.ncbi.nlm.nih.gov/pubmed/25692302
http://www.ncbi.nlm.nih.gov/pubmed/1824543
http://www.ncbi.nlm.nih.gov/pubmed/3022888

Dowdle H. *Confessions of a Cheeseaholic.* Accessed October 2015 from
http://www.vegetariantimes.com/article/confessions-of-a-cheeseaholic/

[4] Peta. December 13, 2010. *Vegans Save 198 Animals a Year.* Accessed May 2014 from
http://www.peta.org/blog/vegans-save-185-animals-year/

[5] Wallace, A. (2011). *Minding Closely The Four Applications of Mindfulness.* Ithaca, New York: Snow Lion Publications.

[6] Farnham A. Oct. 17, 2012. *Seafood From Asia Raised on Pig Waste, Says News Report.* Accessed April 2013 from
http://abcnews.go.com/Business/consumers-eating-feces-tainted-shrimp-fish-seafood-asia/story?id=17491264

[7] Padmakara Translation Group. (2004). *Food of Bodhisattvas.* Boston, MA: Shambala Publications.
Shabkar, entire writing is a reference to vegetarianism.
Atisha, reference to vegetarianism page 76.
Milarepa, reference to vegetarianism page 81.
Khendrup Je, reference to vegetarianism pages 87-88.

Padmakara Translation Group. (1998) *The Words of My Perfect Teacher*. Boston, MA: Shambala Publications. Patrul Rinpoche, reference to vegetarianism pages 53-54, 70-71, 102-105, 190-191, 207-209.

[8] Chen J. (June 4, 2015). *How to Veganize Any Recipe: Sweet Edition.* Accessed at http://vegnews.com/articles/page.do?pageId=5772&catId=2

Chen J. (May 27, 2014). *How to Veganize Any Recipe: Savory Edition.* Accessed at http://vegnews.com/articles/page.do?pageId=5572&catId=2

Parsons R. (November 12, 2014). *How to Veganize Your Favorite Familiar Dishes.* Accessed at http://www.onegreenplanet.org/vegan-food/how-to-veganize-your-favorite-familiar-dishes/

[9] Analytical meditation

Gelek Rimpoche. 1980. *Developing Single-pointed Concentration.* Accessed April 2014 from http://www.lamayeshe.com/article/developing-single-pointed-concentration

Heck J. *How to do analytical meditation.* Accessed April 2014 from http://janheck.com/safe2/HowAnalyticalMed.php

Lee. January 9, 2015. *Importance of Analytical Meditation.* Accessed February 2015 from http://clearemptymind.com/2015/01/09/importance-of-analytical-meditation/

[10] Lam Rim, the graduated path – or roadmap – to enlightenment, is a foundational Buddhist teaching outlining the progression of spiritual practices needed to attain full enlightenment. For more information contact Jewel Heart at http://www.jewelheart.org/digital-dharma/lam-rim-teachings/

[11] Gelek Rimpoche. (1994). Page 34. *Three Principles of the Path.* A Jewel Heart Transcript: http://www.jewelheart.org

[12] Cutler J. & Newland G. (2000). Page 112. *The Great Treatise on the Stages of the Path to Enlightenment (Volume 1).* Ithaca, New York: Snow Lion Publications.

[13] Gelek Rimpoche. (2005). Page 38. *SEM, The Nature of Mind.* A Jewel Heart Transcript. http://www.jewelheart.org

[14] Adams C. (1995) *Neither Man Nor Beast: Feminism and the Defense of Animals.* Page 177. Brooklyn, NY : Lantern Books (Previously Published by New York, NY : Continuum Publishing)

[15] This term was coined by Melanie Joy Ph.D. For more information: www.carnism.org.

[16] Merriam Webster Online Dictionary. Accessed, April 2014 at http://www.merriam-webster.com/dictionary/ethic

[17] Dhammapada, Verses 129-130
http://www.buddha316.com/
http://www.buddhismtoday.com/english/veg/006-animalright-dhammapada.htm
http://www.buddhanet.net/pdf_file/damapada.pdf

[18] Kapleau, Roshi Philip. (1986) To Cherish All Life. Rochester, NY: Rochester Zen Center

[19] A *"rape rack"* is an industry term used to define the apparatus used to hold a dairy cow while she is artificially impregnated.

[20] Thich Nhat Hahn's 14 precepts
http://www.tonglen.oceandrop.org/Thich_Nhat_Hahn_14_Precepts.htm
http://www.mindfulnessbell.org/order_of_interbeing.php

[21] Jewel Heart. Mahayana Precepts. Jewel Heart Blue Prayer book, page 129, www.jewelheart.org

[22] Nagarjuna (c 150-250) was a saintly mystic and scholar from Buddhist India, who lived a few hundred years after the Buddha. He discovered the Mahayana scriptures, was the author of the Madhyamika and founder of the Madhyamika or Middle Way School of tenets.

[23] Gehlek N. (2005). *Lam Rim Teachings, Volume III, Medium Scope*. Page 68, www.jewelheart.org

[24] Eisnitz G. (1997) *Slaughterhouse: The Shocking Story of Greed, Neglect, And Inhumane Treatment Inside the U.S. Meat Industry*. Amherst, NY: Prometheus Books.
Additional resources: To Kill a Chicken
http://www.nytimes.com/2015/03/15/opinion/sunday/nicholas-kristof-to-kill-a-chicken.html?emc=edit_tnt_20150314&nlid=65466980&tntemail0=y&_r=1
Chicken Transport and Slaughter
http://www.peta.org/issues/animals-used-for-food/factory-farming/chickens/chicken-transport-slaughter/

[25] Eisnitz G. (1997) *Slaughterhouse: The Shocking Story of Greed, Neglect, And Inhumane Treatment Inside the U.S. Meat Industry*. Amherst, NY: Prometheus Books.

[26] Buddha Dharma Education Association & Buddhanet. *The Dhammapada The Buddha's Path to Wisdom*. Retrieved from http://www.buddhanet.net/e-learning/buddhism/dp26.htm

[27] Thich Nhat Hahn Fourteen Precepts. Accessed from http://www.tonglen.oceandrop.org/Thich_Nhat_Hahn_14_Precepts.htm

Bromley D. & Hott L. (April 10, 2013). Virginia Commonwealth University. Accessed from http://www.wrs.vcu.edu/profiles/UnifiedBuddhistChurch.htm

[28] Phelps N. (2004). *The Great Compassion.* Page: XIII. Broolyn, NY: Lantern Books.

[29] Campbell T. & Campbell T. (2006). *The China Study: The Most Comprehensive Study of Nutrition Ever Conducted And the Startling Implications for Diet, Weight Loss, And Long-term Health.* Dallas, TX: Benbella Books, Inc.

[30] Joel Fuhrman, M.D. (January 19, 2006). *Nutrient Density of Green Vegetables.*
Accessed from
http://www.diseaseproof.com/archives/healthy-food-nutrient-density-of-green-vegetables.html

[31] Phelps N. (2004). *The Great Compassion.* Page: 156. Broolyn, NY: Lantern Books.

[32] Martin Luther King. Brainy Quote. Accessed from
http://www.brainyquote.com/quotes/quotes/m/martinluth103526.html

[33] Buddha Shakyamuni. Brahmajala Sutra. The Great Middle Way blog. Accessed from
https://greatmiddleway.wordpress.com/2015/09/05/duty/

[34] Dependent origination, in Sanskrit pratityasamutpada, postulates that dependently-related phenomenon are any phenomenon that exist in dependence upon other phenomena. All phenomena are dependently-related because all phenomena depend upon their parts. Dependent origination is pictured in the twelve links of the Wheel of Life. It is a form of the theory of relativity 2,500 years prior to Einstein's, general and special theories. All things dependently arise. All are related and connected.

[35] Lopez Jr. D. & Buswell Jr. R. (May 15, 2014). 10 Misconceptions about Buddhism: Beggars Can't Be

Choosers, The Buddha explicitly rejected vegetarianism as a requirement for his followers. Accessed from http://www.tricycle.com/blog/beggars-can%E2%80%99t-be-choosers

36 Wikipedia. Accessed, May 2014, at
http://en.wikipedia.org/wiki/Sramana
Merriam Webster Online Dictionary. Accessed, May 2014, at http://www.merriam-webster.com/dictionary/sramana

37 The Huffington Post. (July 18, 2013). *Luiz Antonio, Adorable Child, Sums Up Moral Argument For Being Vegetarian As Only A Kid Can (VIDEO).*
http://www.huffingtonpost.com/2013/05/31/luiz-antonio-vegetarian-where-meat-comes-from_n_3366242.html
Luiz Antonio on YouTube:
https://www.youtube.com/watch?v=CHABgTqqrz0

38 Kyabje Lama Thubten Zopa Rinpoche. (May 22, 1987). *Purifying with the Four Powers.*
Accessed at
https://www.lamayeshe.com/index.php?sect=article&id=810

39 Buddhist Text Translation Society. Accessed at
http://www.fodian.net/world/1484.html

40 Gelek Rimpoche. (1998). *Odyssey to Freedom in Sixty-Four Steps.* Page 48. www.jewelheart.org

41 Gelek Rimpoche. (1998). *Odyssey to Freedom in Sixty-Four Steps.* Day Three, Step 7, Purify all that is negative. Page 47. www.jewelheart.org

42 Benson J. (September 22, 2013). *Toxic glyphosate (Roundup) found to be harming dairy cows.* Accessed at
http://www.naturalnews.com/042175_glyphosate_dairy_cows_harmful_effects.html

43 Farm Sancturary. *Chickens Used for Eggs. Chickens Used for Meat.* Accessed at http://www.farmsanctuary.org/learn/factory-farming/chickens/

44 Farm Sanctuary. *Queenie: Daring NYC Cow Makes a Dash for Freedom.* Accessed at http://www.farmsanctuary.org/the-sanctuaries/rescued-animals/featured-past-rescues/queenie/

45 Christian Cotroneo. (06/13/2014). *Pig Jumps From Truck Bound For Slaughterhouse (VIDEO).* Accessed at http://www.huffingtonpost.ca/2014/06/13/pig-jumps-truck-slaughterhouse_n_5492571.html

Mercy for Our Sentients. (May 29, 2009). *I am scared and don't want to die.* Accessed at https://www.youtube.com/watch?v=LUkHkyy4uqw

46 Michael Greger, M.D. (October 9th 2015). *Cholesterol and Alzheimer's Disease.* Accessed at http://nutritionfacts.org/video/cholesterol-and-alzheimers-disease/

Michael Greger, M.D. (September 25th 2015). Alzheimer's and Atherosclerosis of the Brain. Accessed at http://nutritionfacts.org/video/alzheimers-and-atherosclerosis-of-the-brain/

47 Wikipedia. *World population estimates.* Accessed at https://en.wikipedia.org/wiki/World_population_estimates

Ecology Global Network. *Population Estimates: Year One through 2050 A.D.* Accessed at http://www.ecology.com/population-estimates-year-2050/

Worldometers. *World Population.* Accessed at http://www.worldometers.info/world-population/

Our World in Data. World Population Growth. Accessed at http://ourworldindata.org/data/population-growth-vital-statistics/world-population-growth/

NOVA Science Programming on Air and Online. *Human Numbers Through Time.* Accessed at http://www.pbs.org/wgbh/nova/worldbalance/numb-nf.html

Smil V. (December 2011). Population and Development Review. *Harvesting the Biosphere: The Human Impact.* Accessed at http://www.vaclavsmil.com/wp-content/uploads/PDR37-4.Smil_.pgs613-636.pdf

[48] A Well-Fed World. *Factory Farms.* Accessed at http://awfw.org/factory-farms/

Animals Deserve Absolute Protection Today and Tomorrow (ADAPTT). (2-10-15) *More Than 150 Billion Animals Slaughtered Every Year.* Accessed at http://www.adaptt.org/killcounter.html

[49] Ross P. (November 26, 2013) *Cow Farts Have 'Larger Greenhouse Gas Impact' Than Previously Thought; Methane Pushes Climate Change.* International Business Times. Accessed at http://www.ibtimes.com/cow-farts-have-larger-greenhouse-gas-impact-previously-thought-methane-pushes-climate-change-1487502

Shindell D., Faluvegi G., Koch D., Schmidt G., Unger N., Bauer S. (October 30, 2009). *Improved Attribution of Climate Forcing to Emissions.* Accessed at http://www.sciencemag.org/content/326/5953/716.figures-only

[50] Rainforest Relief. *Avoiding Unsustainable Rainforest Wood.* Accessed at http://www.rainforestrelief.org/What_to_Avoid_and_Alternatives/Rainforest_Wood.html

Save The Rainforest. *Facts about the rainforest.* Accessed at http://www.savetherainforest.org/savetherainforest_007.htm

Rain Tree. (12-21-2012). *Rainforest Facts.* Accessed at
http://www.rain-tree.com/facts.htm

Reid W. & Miller K. (Oct. 1989). Keeping Options Alive: The
Scientific Basis for Conserving Biodiversity. Accessed at
http://pdf.wri.org/keepingoptionsalive_bw.pdf

[51] Thornton P. & Herrero M. & Ericksen P. (November 2011).
Livestock and climate change. Accessed at
https://cgspace.cgiar.org/bitstream/handle/10568/10601
/IssueBrief3.pdf

Smith P., M. Bustamante, H. Ahammad, H. Clark, H. Dong,
E.A. Elsiddig, H. Haberl, R. Harper, J. House, M. Jafari,
O. Masera, C. Mbow, N.H. Ravindranath, C.W. Rice, C.
Robledo Abad, A. Romanovskaya, F. Sperling, and F.
Tubiello, 2014: Agriculture, Forestry and Other Land
Use (AFOLU). In: Climate Change 2014: Mitigation of
Climate Change. Contribution of Working Group III to
the Fifth Assessment Report of the Intergovernmental
Panel on Climate Change [Edenhofer, O., R. Pichs-
Madruga, Y. Sokona, E. Farahani, S. Kadner, K. Seyboth,
A. Adler, I. Baum, S. Brunner, P. Eickemeier, B.
Kriemann, J. Savolainen, S. Schlömer, C. von Stechow,
T. Zwickel and J.C. Minx (eds.)]. Cambridge University
Press, Cambridge, United Kingdom and New York, NY,
USA.Accessed at
http://www.ipcc.ch/pdf/assessment-
report/ar5/wg3/ipcc_wg3_ar5_chapter11.pdf

[52] Saka Dawa:

FPMT. *Taking the Eight Mahayana Precepts.* Accessed at
http://fpmt.org/prayers/taking-the-eight-mahayana-
precepts/

Sera Mey Monastic University. *SAKA DAWA (the Full Moon
Day).* Accessed at
http://serameymonastery.org/SakaDawa.aspx

Drepung Gomang Monastery. (2012). *HOLY SAKA DAWA
MONTH.* Accessed at

http://drepunggomang.org/curriculum/9-uncategorised/98-holy-saka-dawa-month

Shantideva Meditation NYC. *Saka Dawa Practice Day.* Accessed at http://shantidevameditation.org/saka-dawa-2014/?doing_wp_cron=1444852577.08463311195373 53515625

Huff Post Religion (5/05/2012). *Vesak: How Buddha's Birthday Is Celebrated Around The World (PHOTOS).* Accessed at http://www.huffingtonpost.com/2012/05/05/vesak-how-buddhas-birthda_n_1478896.html

Smith L. (May 27, 2015). *Vesak Day: How the birth, enlightenment and death of the Buddha is celebrated.* International Business Times. Accessed at http://www.ibtimes.co.uk/vesak-day-how-birth-enlightenment-death-buddha-celebrated-1503141

Yowangdu. (May 5, 2013). *Saka Dawa: A Month Honoring the Buddha's Life.* Accessed at http://www.yowangdu.com/tibetan-buddhism/saka-dawa.html

O'Brien B. Saga Dawa or Saka Dawa Holy Month for Tibetan Buddhists. Accessed at http://buddhism.about.com/od/buddhistholidays/fl/Saga-Dawa-or-Saka-Dawa.htm

[53] The Vegan Society. Definition of veganism. Accessed at https://www.vegansociety.com/try-vegan/definition-veganism

[54] Luke. *The Vegan Calculator.* The Vegan Web Designer. Accessed at http://thevegancalculator.com/#calculator

34318272R20084

Made in the USA
San Bernardino, CA
25 May 2016